JThe ustice Story

TRUE TALES OF
murder,
mystery,
mayhem

Compiled and Edited by
Joseph McNamara

Publisher: Joseph J. Bannon Jr.
Managing Editor: Michelle Summers
Dustjacket Design: Terry Neutz Hayden
Photo Editors: Eric Meskauskas and Angela Troisi
Proofreader/Copyeditor: David Hamburg

ISBN: 1-58261-285-4
Library of Congress Catalog Card Number: 00-101371

Bannon Multimedia Group
www.BMGpub.com

Printed in the United States

In Memoriam

Joe McNamara, a newspaper legend, signed off the other night and took with him a huge chunk of the heart and the history of the *Daily News*. Joe Mac, as he was universally known, died in Summit, N.J., on May 15, 2000, after a long, rewarding career writing about murder, mystery and mayhem.

For the past 17 years, he was the gentle soul behind "The Justice Story," the celebrated, long-running Sunday feature about notorious real-life crimes.

His own life was a remarkable contrast. White-haired, soft-spoken and eternally unflappable, Joe looked like he wouldn't harm a flea—and he wouldn't.

When he took over "The Justice Story" in 1983, McNamara was already an expert on true crime, having sold more than 200 stories to various magazines.

"He made it look so easy," said former *Daily News* editor Gil Spencer. "I used to sit and watch him work, like you watch anybody who's the best at what he does."

McNamara is survived by his wife of 49 years, Josephine Hanley McNamara; six children, Diane Irving, Kathleen Deeken, Michael McNamara, Ellen Ambrose, Virginia Harris and Patrick McNamara; five brothers and sisters; and 18 grandchildren.

—Daily News
May 17, 2000

Table of Contents

Mayhem

Introduction

Ever since Cain, in a jealous rage, killed his brother Abel at the dawn of time, mankind has been shocked, revolted and fascinated by crime and the violence one can visit upon another. Cain, a farmer, was resentful that the sacrifices of his shepherd brother were more worthy in the eyes of God. And Cain was justly punished, cast out to roam the earth a vagabond and fugitive.

Jealousy looms very large in the history of murder. It is a most powerful emotion. Sex and greed may very well account for most other slayings. But not all motives for murder are so clear-cut. Indeed, some are never known. And even that mystery adds something to the tale.

In smoky caves the storyteller's account of violence entranced our ancestors as fearful shadows etched the walls and animals stirred outside—like Cain.

Fairy tales are rife with violence and terror, and the young for centuries have relished them, though in truth the Brothers Grimm collected the folk tales for adults. It shows that injustice and cruelty do not sway the listener or reader from a gripping story.

In this volume of "Justice Stories" taken from the files of the *Daily News* you will meet a wide array of miscreants.

You may know Fritz Haarmann, the butchering "Werewolf of Hanover." If you don't, you should. Vivian Gordon, the lovely, red-haired Courtesan of Broadway, is worth a read.

Ed Gein is here. A mama's boy and ghoulish headhunter in Wisconsin during the 1950s, Ed caught the interest of filmmaker Alfred Hitchcock, who immortalized this strange duck in *Psycho*.

You'll meet Adolph Louis Luetgert. You don't know him? You will. He was a Chicago sausage maker of some repute, a 250-pounder who discovered sex early in life and decided it was for him. When his wife, Louise, protested the steady stream of luscious bimbos, Luetgert hit upon a novel solution to his problems, he thought.

And Jim Fisk, the fabled industrialist of bygone years, is set upon on the scarlet staircase of one of New York City's most luxurious hotels.

Ah, yes, they're all here, the vicious, the vain, the outrageous, even the pitiful, who have slithered, stalked, paraded and stormed through the "Justice Stories" of the *Daily News* for more than three-quarters of a century, just the way the *Daily News* founder Joseph Patterson would have liked it. After all, "The Justice Story" was his idea.

Times may change, as they certainly have since Patterson's day. Man may become more sophisticated. Travel may improve; medicine may lengthen life. But man's nature, which provides the motive for his crimes, has it changed? Hardly. Remember Cain?

During the 1930s, the Golden Age of Radio, there was a crime program called "The Shadow." At one point, a man's voice, slightly echoed and with sufficient menace, would intone, "Who knows what evil lurks in the hearts of men?"

Readers of these original "Justice Stories" know. And now, you, too can know.

Joseph McNamara

Murder

Below is the first weekly "Justice Story" to appear in the Daily News, *on May 6, 1923. Bearing no byline, and only the headline "What Has Happened to Justice?" it detailed the slaying of Joseph Elwell, noted Manhattan gambler, expert on bridge whist, gourmet and avid skirt chaser.*

A vain man, he had 40 wigs and a voluminous love index file of beautiful women.

He also had an enemy.

What Has Happened to Justice?

Joseph Bowne Elwell, enemy of men and of women, was found dying in the reception hall of his home at 244 W. 70th St., Manhattan. It was a "woman's crime," agreed every leading detective of the country, including the chief of the United States Secret Service. The stars invoked through astrology disagreed as to the actual slayer, but conceded that a woman was present, that she formed the guiding influence.

But which woman?

The very multiplicity of the feminine associations of the man supplied a safety zone to any one of them.

For in the Elwell home, a four-story house of fine location and beautiful furnishing, it was reported there were found photographs of 1,000 women. A card index system—showing 53 of the fair sex who had smiled upon the master, given their charms and received largesse from his means—told what story it might.

And yet there is no word of proof to show that the crime was "a woman's trick." Elwell, the known master of bridge whist, a shark who used his vast skill to the undoing of men, was also a racehorse owner and gambler, as well as a fringe-grabber on the edge of that night society which skirts the real social realm, just as Broadway and the cross streets cling about the skirts of Fifth Avenue and the exclusive section beyond.

For matter of motive, there existed any quantity of reasons to pick a man as the slinking criminal who, just after the postman handed Elwell his mail at 7:35 on the morning of June 11, 1920, fired a heavy .45 caliber bullet from an automatic through the gambler's forehead. But 55 brief minutes intervened between the time when Elwell was known to be alive and read a letter from his trainer in Kentucky and 8:30 of the same morning when Marie Larsen, his housekeeper, found the stricken man, desperately wounded, unable to speak, crouched in a big chair in the reception hall of his home. Three hours later, in Bellevue Hospital, he died.

It is essential to know something of the habits of the man. Elwell had been separated from his wife for four years. Helen Derby Elwell and her son, Richard Derby Elwell, then 15, had no apparent relation with him other than to draw a portion of the royalties from his whist writings, which were accepted the world over as authority.

Elwell had thrown himself into the night life of the city, the carefree life of Palm Beach, and into the quicksands of indiscriminate association with women. He garnered many a one in his net, not that he possessed any superior attraction, but on the principle that any man with nerve, good legs and persistent effort may sell many mousetraps in the course of a month if he boldly pursues his mission. And Elwell was known as "a quick canvasser" with women. He accosted them in the streets as he rode in his automobile, he took a chance in the cafes and roof shows and thus he came to amass his remarkable collection of pictures and names, most of which told silent stories of indiscretion.

They were women of every walk—the society woman who came to know him as a bridge teacher and master, or, who in a flight of her own, esteemed him a safe outlet for a vagrant spasm of relaxation; the divorcee seeking consolation; the shopgirl who was dazzled by the glamor of a man who made his $150,000 estate scintillate more than most of the millionaires; the frothy stage woman of the passing period; all shades and varieties of femininity came to his net.

And still there seemed to be no one bound to him by a tie of affection, and not one came to see him buried. Two elderly women, faces lined by the passing of many years and surely immune from any possible question, made up the sole feminine contingent as the body was lowered into the grave, aside from the five persons who belonged, intimately, to his family life. So the motive of a real love's making—common in murder cases—was lost in the sea of frilled charmers who played fleeting parts in his life tragedy.

Only a mysterious young blonde, clad in black, who flitted in and out of the house two years after his death, supposedly taking something from a hiding place under the floor of a closet next to his bedroom, has come since the murder to supply a hint. And she came with two men, scouted the lay of the land, returned alone and got away without being identified, carrying whatever telltale article she found under a long cape. The house had then passed into the hands of another owner and was for rent. She came as a prospective tenant, and departed like some wraith.

Examining, in the light of three years of collected effort on the part of detectives and officials, the thread of the story increases rather than loses its interest. There had been nothing in Elwell's routine up to the evening preceding the murder to attract attention. Then he appeared at dinner at the Ritz with Mr. and Mrs. Walter Lewisohn, Viola Kraus, sister of Mrs. Lewisohn, and Octnvio Figuero, a South American newspaperman.

Parenthetically, Viola had been married to Victor von Schlegel. They had been divorced, and the final decree received its time-bearing effect on the very day of the dinner. From the Ritz, the party went to the Ziegfeld Roof. Fate, taking small account of individuals, led to the Ziegfeld Victor von Schlegel, the divorced husband, in company with Emily Hope Anderson, a charming young woman of Minneapolis.

Von Schlegel nodded to the company as he went to his own table. At the time, no one knew the name of his companion, and in the days of search that followed the crime, she was "The Mysterious Woman in Black" until events served to remove the mystery. All was gaiety on the Roof. There was no hint of trouble. At the close of the fiesta, the Elwell party went to the street, where Lewisohn offered to drive Elwell home in his car.

"I would prefer to walk," he said, and started toward Seventh Avenue.

But Elwell apparently changed his mind, for he went, not home, but to the Café Montmartre at Broadway and 50th Street.

Two men and a woman sat with him at a table, engaged in conversation.

It was shortly before 2 a.m. when Elwell left the Roof. He remained an hour and a half in the cafe with his three companions. Then a man drove him home in a small and noisy roadster and dropped him at the door. Identity of the man is unknown.

Elwell lived on the third floor of his house, in a room that was filled with rare bits of art. Adjoining his own room was one furnished in exquisite style, and set with every property that might be either necessary or pleasing for a woman. Yet no one woman ever lived in that house. They came, remained at times for hours and then went away. Some of them came often, one so often as to be noticed.

And yet Justice never found any of his intimates for questioning.

Returning to our mutton, Elwell went, evidently, to his room, removed his evening clothes, in which $400 in bills was found, discounting the notion of a burglar's visit, changed to pajamas and went downstairs to the reception hall to the telephone. There at 4:30 in the morning, he called Far Rockaway 1841, the home of W.H. Pendleton, at Lawrence, L.I. He got no response. Night was day and day was night with this man, and there is nothing peculiar in the fact that at 6:09 a.m. the telephone records show that he called for a number at Garden City.

But it *is* strange that while the first call was so accurately reported the next day, nobody has yet heard what number he wanted at Garden City, nor has the name of the owner of the telephone reached the light of day.

The milkman, calling at 6:45, found the outside front door unlocked.

The postman, bringing letters at 7:35, found the door still unlocked.

One of the letters he brought was from Kentucky, from Elwell's trainer, and it was evident that he was alive when it arrived, for when they found him crouched in the big chair, the open letter was still near his hand. Larsen, the housekeeper, did not live on the premises, and it was 8:30 when she entered to find her master shot.

Straight and true through the forehead went the shot, passing entirely through the head and burying itself an inch in the wall behind. Amateur sleuths, viewing the directness of the aim, said an expert shot did the job. Nonsense! Pistol shooting is the most natural of arts, and one who points a gun as though it were a warning finger rarely misses.

A long line of shooting women who shot dead to the mark give proof that it is the untrained woman with a pistol who gets her man, where dead shots have emptied their weapons across a narrow street without a hit.

All New York was agog with the mystery. Viola Kraus was known to have been a friend of Elwell's. Had he not her picture in his room?

The investigation started with a grilling of Viola and her former husband. Von Schlegel showed that he went to Atlantic City by motor after the roof party and could not have been involved. Kraus satisfied the officials as to her own course, and then flitted away to Paris to establish an industry of her own in that city of fancy and fable.

"A Mysterious Woman in White," identified as Mrs. James Wilmerding, prominent in society, was dragged into the case over the line of a servant's talk, and her name was cleared in short order.

No trace of the two men and the woman with whom he passed his last hours at the Café Montmartre—

No trace of the man who drove him home—

No trace of the missing Garden City call.

S. Rudomini, a locksmith at 184 West End Ave., reported that he had made three keys to the front door. One he gave to Edward Rhodes, Elwell's chauffeur, and the other two *were placed under the mat of the front door.*

It was not only a door with "Welcome" on the mat, but a door that had before its hospitable stretch a key waiting under the mat for such as knew the habits of the owner and the location of the key. Any of the 53 card-indexed sirens who passed in and out of his life surely had knowledge of the cache of the sesame that led inside.

"A woman," said famed detective William J. Burns.

And all the other sleuths echoed, "A woman," but Justice stopped short at the formidable array of the fair that confronted the blind goddess, hesitating which way to turn. As to the woman who came, two years after the crime, to delve in the old closet, she came to the house one afternoon with two men. She said that she was "Miss Bowne of New Orleans, living at the Hotel Ansonia." Bowne was Elwell's middle name, you recall.

The caretaker took the trio through the house. They paused nowhere until they reached the third floor. Then they inspected the closet. One of the men tapped the matting with his cane. The caretaker heard him whisper:

"Hollow, sure enough."

Then they went away. The next day the blonde in black came alone. She asked to see the third floor again, slipped the caretaker a $5 note and ran lightly up the stairs. The caretaker following leisurely, encountered her on the steps coming down. She held her long cape about her form as though concealing something. She went away, he told the police, and that was the last of the blonde in black.

Bloody Boudoir

JOSEPH MCNAMARA
JULY 19, 1998

A staccato of gunshots erupted in a handsome ranch home early that hot Sunday morn, and Benita Lebow, visiting parents across the street, bolted upright in bed. A man screamed, "Help! Help! Somebody help me!"

And then the crash of more gunfire.

Lebow phoned police, who raced to the house at 610 NE 171st St., North Miami Beach. It was the home of Robert Wilbur Ball Sr., 48, a millionaire builder and scion of a prominent family.

On the living room floor lay Ball, badly wounded, his dark blue suit soaked with blood.

"Look at the people in the bedroom," he groaned.

In the bloodied bedroom lay a nude and dead couple—Regina Ball, 33, the builder's beautiful brunette wife, and her lover, Daniel de Lloyd Nash, 36.

Regina, a former cocktail waitress, was shot in the chest and back. Nash, a Miami hoodlum with a gambling/bookmaking record, had picked up three slugs in what was obviously a furious shootout with .38s. An empty .38 lay near Nash's body.

One of Nash's slugs grazed Ball's cheek. Another crippled one of his fingers. A third struck him in the right leg. A fourth broke his left arm and entered his armpit. A fifth and sixth lodged near his spine.

As Ball was wheeled out of the recovery room in North Miami General Hospital, he asked Robert Ball Jr., a son by a previous marriage, "Did she die?" He obviously referred to his petite wife of three years. But the son, cautioned by his father's lawyer, Max Lurie, did not answer.

Ball was charged with two counts of homicide.

The boudoir gun duel, at 6:50 a.m. Aug. 1, 1965, electrified the Miami area. Aside from the violence and drama, Ball's family was big in town. His father, Le Grand "Lee" Ball, was a founder of the Seaquarium, a tourist attraction, and a member of the Social Register.

The gun-toting son, along with his building income, commanded the proceeds of a $2.5 million trust fund.

Ball had met Regina Darlene McCormack at the Cypress Lounge on NW Seventh Ave., where she served drinks. A divorcee, she had a son, Steven, from a former marriage. The boy, then four, was visiting relatives in Texas when the gunfire flared in the bedroom.

They might have seemed an unlikely pair, fat, fretful Ball and his tiny wife with a shape that wouldn't quit. But they wed in 1962, and despite their 15-year age difference, they seemed happy enough, at first. Then came the quarrels, often and loud.

A year after the wedding, there were divorce proceedings. Then a reconciliation. At that point, Ball adopted Steven as his own.

Trouble again flared in paradise, and in December 1964 Regina Ball once more sued for divorce, charging cruelty. A month later a judge issued a restraining order against Ball. And in May 1965 he was jailed for several days after Regina said he beat her when he ran into her in a tavern.

A final divorce hearing, set for mid-July 1965, was postponed when Ball was hospitalized after an auto crash. He recovered and was living at No. 1 Sunset Isle at the time of the shooting.

Police described Nash, a co-owner of a Miami boat company, as unsavory, an associate of local hoodlums. Further, he had been in some trouble with the law in his native New Jersey.

"It was self-defense," Ball said of the shooting. "Nash fired first."

"Nonsense," snapped Gerald Kogan, assistant state attorney. "It was murder in the first degree. Ball fired eight shots. Three hit Nash, two hit Mrs. Ball. Three went wild in the bedroom. And there were three live bullets in his gun. Obviously, he reloaded his six-shooter. And that's premeditation."

The Dade County grand jury indicted Ball on two counts of first-degree murder, and he went on trial in October 1966. The state hoped to prove that Ball committed a felony when he broke into the house on NE 171st St. to commit another felony. The double felony, if proved, could mean the death penalty.

But Judge Francis Christie ruled that Ball could not "break into" a house he owned.

A neighbor testified she saw Nash and Regina Ball enter the house half an hour before the shooting. Others testified they had seen Nash's Cadillac in front of the house for about a week.

The state charged that Ball first shot his wife and fired at Nash as the hoodlum went for his gun. Ball then took the stand, his body jerking with sobs.

"I didn't intend to hit Regina," he said. "I still wanted her. I would have taken her back in spite of all this. I had my gun in my pocket when I went in."

Ball insisted that despite court orders, his wife had invited him over 12 or 14 times during their separation. She wanted to reconcile, he declared. He quoted her as saying, "That fellow from New Jersey is pretty rotten. . . . If I break up with him, he will bury you."

"That's why I bought the gun," said Ball. "I saw Regina Saturday night, and she said to come by the house early next morning . . . but not if his [Nash's] car was parked outside. His car wasn't parked there."

That fateful morning, Ball slid aside four jalousie panels in a porch window and slipped into the dining room. He went to the bedroom. As Ball related it:

"They were sitting cross-legged at the foot of the bed, smoking, without a stitch of clothes. I said to the man, 'Put your clothes on and leave. I want to talk to my wife.' The man said to Regina, 'I'll take care of him,' and from somewhere he started shooting.

"The first shot hit me in the stomach. I said, 'Please leave. I'll explain this [apparently to police].' Then he shot me again."

Ball yanked his own pistol. He testified:

"It seemed like a hundred years when I pulled that hammer back. I remember screaming at the door for help. I knew if I didn't get help, somebody would die. I thought he would murder me. I wanted to leave the door open so somebody would see me if I fell. I don't remember going to the car [as the state charged]. I don't remember reloading."

Asked about a neighbor's testimony of a two-to-five-minute interval between bursts of shooting, Ball said, "I don't remember."

A private-duty nurse, Gail McCue, testified she overheard Ball say at the hospital that the only reason he was not dead was that Nash was so drunk, he could not shoot straight.

Another witness quoted Ball as saying he had told Nash politely, "This is my home and I want you to get out." In fact, the defense made much of the "reasonable" Ball approach.

Defense attorney Nicholas Capuano went so far as to surmise that Ball had been coming to see her about a trip to Texas together and that Nash meant to shoot him dead—but had not figured on Ball having a pistol.

Kogan, in summation, discounted this theory. Slipping on the blue coat Ball wore at the shooting, Kogan tried to shove Ball's .38 into a pocket. It did not fit. On this dramatic note, the state rested.

The jury convicted Ball on two counts of second-degree murder. Christie sentenced him to two life terms, to run concurrently.

Over a prosecution objection, Ball was released on $25,000 bond, pending appeal. While out, he was bagged March 31, 1967, in the $10,000 robbery of a West Palm Beach woman. However, this action was not pressed when Ball's murder-trial appeal was denied, and he was hiked off to state prison.

In mid-1972, after having served five years for the fatal bedroom shooting of his wife and her lover, Ball was released on parole. He went to Nevada to fulfill the Florida Parole Commission proviso that he leave the Sunshine State.

Butchering Beast

JOSEPH MCNAMARA
DECEMBER 15, 1996

As loathsome, murderous ogres go, Fritz Haarmann went pretty far. His slaughter of teenage youths satisfied a perverted sex drive and made him considerable money, what with meat being so short in the Germany of post-World War I. He even sold his victims' clothes.

Townfolk called him "The Werewolf of Hanover." Some criminologists label him the greatest monster of his time.

Haarmann was born in Hanover on Oct. 25, 1879, the youngest of six children of railroad fireman Olle Haarmann. A brother of Haarmann's was sent to prison for assaulting a 12-year-old girl. His three sisters were hookers.

Early on, Haarmann became the pet of his invalid mother, playing with dolls and wearing dresses. At 16 he was sent to a military school but was dismissed after an epileptic attack.

Back home, Haarmann worked in a cigar factory his father had started, but he was accused of molesting small children and was sent to an asylum for the feeble-minded. He escaped to Switzerland.

Haarmann returned to Hanover in 1900 and became engaged. When he discovered he had made his fiancée pregnant, he enlisted in the army.

He was discharged in 1903 for neurasthenia (nervous exhaustion) and returned to Hanover, where he became a thief. He was hit with many small jail terms.

Dad tried to set Haarmann up in a fish-and-chips place, but it folded. Becoming a warehouse packer, he stole so much that in 1914 he was sentenced to prison.

The elder Haarmann, whom the younger hated, tried to have his son committed, but experts determined that while a bit off the wall, the young man was not crazy.

Now, at 39, Haarmann discovered his life's work. Germany, racked by the war, suffered many shortages, including meat. Haarmann became a butcher and wormed his way into a smuggling ring that provided many of the scarce items.

In this quagmire of social unrest, youths were constantly on the move seeking jobs and something to eat. They hung around the railroad station and nearby marketplace, where Haarmann hawked his bootleg meat. He took lodgings conveniently nearby at 27 Cellarstrasse.

At the same time, Haarmann became a police informer, and the law overlooked many of his indiscretions to avoid losing him as a snitch.

Haarmann's technique was simple. He would roam the station area or marketplace, promising the tender needy a warm meal and a place to sleep. Those who accepted the offer of the amiable-looking Haarmann were never seen alive again.

Haarmann's first victim was runaway Friedel Rothe, 17, whom he picked up Sept. 27, 1918. Two days after Rothe ran away from home, his father came back from the front and searched for him. A friend of the youth reported he had seen the boy with a "detective." Haarmann often passed himself off as a detective.

Cops paid a surprise visit to Haarmann's digs and found him with a youth, not Rothe. By this time, Rothe was dead—his head wrapped in newspaper and lying behind Haarmann's stove. Lawmen rummaging through Haarmann's quarters never found it.

Haarmann was given nine months in jail for indecency, but police pressed no further into Rothe's disappearance.

Released in September 1919, Fritz met Hans Grans, a 24-year-old thief and pimp. They became lovers and partners in Haarmann's gruesome business. Youths began vanishing frequently. For a while, Haarmann maintained an average of a murder every two weeks, though he killed as often as twice in one day.

On one occasion Haarmann killed a youth because Grans wanted the victim's pants.

Between 1918 and 1923, there was no record of Haarmann's bloody work—the Rothe case was the only one police investigated. But after February 1923, details were available: a Fritz Franke, 17, who vanished on Feb. 12; Wilhelm Schurze, 17, on March 20; Roland Huch, 16, on May 23; Hans Sennefeld, 20, that same month.

On and on the list went, in sickening detail. Not long after the Franke slaying, two prostitute friends of Grans' visited 27 Cellarstrasse while the men were out. The women saw several pots of meat and provided police with some of it. A police expert reported the meat was pork.

While the body of only one victim was ever recovered, the clothing of the slain was traced later to Haarmann or to Grans. One coat was found on a son of Haarmann's landlady.

The one body found, in a canal tied and strangled, was of Hans Keimes, a handsome 17-year-old who vanished May 17, 1924. When family members reported Keimes missing, Haarmann went to see them. He asked to see a photo of the youth and promised the family that if the boy were in Hanover, he would find him in three days.

Then Haarmann went to the police and accused Grans of killing Keimes. The two creeps had been fighting bitterly over some of the victims' clothing. But Grans showed lawmen that at the time of the crime, he had been in jail for a minor offense.

Police strangely made no attempt to tie the Keimes slaying to Haarmann. The litany of killings went on. In fact, it was not detective work that halted the blood orgy. It was sheer accident.

On May 17—the day Keimes disappeared—children playing on the banks of the Leine River found a human skull. Two weeks later, a smaller skull was found downriver. On June 13, two more skulls were spotted in the mud.

After an investigation, the police surgeon concluded that some medical students were playing a joke. Other cops disagreed, though, and two detectives from Berlin were assigned to watch Haarmann.

At 2 a.m. on June 22, Haarmann was spotted prowling among sleeping youths outside the station. A spat developed. Haarmann rushed to a police post and demanded that a youth named Fromm be arrested for traveling without a ticket. Fromm, in turn, accused Haarmann of indecency. Both were hiked off to headquarters for investigation.

A thorough search of Haarmann's digs turned up clothing and articles later traced to some of the missing youths. Bloodstained walls, earlier attributed to Haarmann's unlicensed butchering, now took on a more ominous aspect to the police.

On July 24, a sackful of whitened bones and another skull were found in the Leine, and the residents of Hanover went bonkers. Newspapers reported that in 1924 alone, 600 youths ages 14 to 16 had vanished.

Police dragged the river and found 500 additional human bones.

In the face of public panic and wrath, police now grilled Haarmann and wrung a confession from him. He called Grans an instigator and accomplice in the heinous crimes. With icy hauteur, Grans refused to talk.

Charged with 27 counts of murder, the Werewolf of Hanover went to trial in December 1924.

During the proceedings, the defendant puffed cigars grandly and complained there were too many women in the courtroom.

The prosecution immediately poked holes in the defense's planned insanity plea by putting on the stand three eminent doctors who ruled that while Haarmann was inferior mentally, he was not irresponsible under the definition of the law. The defense collapsed.

Haarmann was convicted and sentenced to die.

Grans was found guilty as an accomplice in the ghastly slayings and was sentenced to life in prison. This term was later reduced to 12 years.

The Werewolf, strange by anyone's yardstick, expressed indignation that only 27 slayings had been included in his indictment and trial.

He said the number was actually nearer to 40, though he "could not say definitely."

On the morning of April 15, 1925, Fritz Haarmann was beheaded.

Candlelight Killer
Was Stoked by Madness

JOSEPH MCNAMARA
MAY 31, 1987

There are times when the ways of justice are very strange and are served by the most extraordinary of surrogates.

Robert W. Liberty was known as the Candlelight Killer from the time he was found strumming his guitar as he sat alongside the strangled body of his girlfriend, lighted candles burning at the head and foot of her makeshift bier. This was June 4, 1966. Liberty, then 19, had met Marcella Landis, 31, while both were in a medical center in California, recovering from suicide attempts.

After their release, the thin-faced Liberty, whose only talent up to then had been glue-sniffing, went to live with Landis, who was estranged from her husband. They took an apartment in Westminster, a small community southeast of Los Angeles.

For no special reason, Liberty used a silk stocking on Landis that Saturday in June, then dressed her, applied eye make-up and laid her out on a couch with a Bible on her chest and the burning tapers at feet and head. He called police and waited.

Back into custody went Liberty, but two months after his ritualistic slaying, three court-appointed psychiatrists disagreed on his sanity. On Aug. 26, 1966, Orange County judge Robert Gardner sided with the majority and declared Liberty legally insane. He was sent to Atascadero State Hospital for 90 days or until he could assist in his own defense.

The following February, Liberty was back in court. He was found not guilty of the Landis murder on his plea of insanity and Judge Byron McMillan committed him to Vacaville State Hospital for the Criminally Insane on May 9, 1967. McMillan said psychiatrists indicated Liberty was still dangerous.

Moved to Metropolitan State Hospital in Nowalk, Liberty was found by psychiatrists two years later to have recovered, and a hearing was set in June 1969 to establish his sanity. An embarrassed hospital official, Dr. Fred Linder, explained that Liberty had walked out of the hospital June 2, and a week later, in error, a typist marked him discharged.

The doctor admitted Liberty was still missing, but he hastily assured the court that the mislaid patient was now regarded sane— though he could be dangerous if he used drugs or liquor.

Three weeks later, the Candlelight Killer surfaced at the office of his attorney. He thought he had been released and had been visiting friends in Oregon. Told by his mother he was wanted by police, Liberty surrendered. He was taken to the Orange County Medical Center for evaluation, and on Sept. 15, six psychiatrists agreed with Linder that Liberty was sane, but could be dangerous if he drank or used drugs.

On the basis of this, the district attorney asked that the patient be kept in custody. Judge Gardner replied that speculation was not enough, that under the law, he had to free the Candlelight Killer.

So Liberty wandered to the community of Costa Mesa and moved into an apartment with three men. On March 12, 1970, one of the buddies, Thomas C. Astorina, 25, a father of two, was found dead in a ditch in Huntington Beach. He had been shot in the stomach with a .22 pistol and left to die.

Though there were no candles, no guitar strumming, Liberty was accused of the slaying and police throughout California and the FBI searched for him. He was next spotted in Long Beach on June 6 when Richard Greytak, 17, made the mistake of picking up a hitchhiker and his girlfriend. Once in the car, Liberty yanked a .22 pistol and forced Greytak to drive him and his companion, Kendall Ann Bierly, 24, to Westminster, Calif.

There, Liberty convinced his mother she owed him $45— most of the persuasion done with the .22. Then Greytak was forced to drive the pair to San Diego, to the apartment of one Robert Orion, 53, a male nurse in a local convalescent home. Liberty and Orion had met while both were incarcerated mental patients.

Tying up Greytak, Liberty beat Orion to death and stole his belongings. He paused long enough to arrange the body on the floor and light candles at the feet and head. On a closet door he scrawled: "The Candlelight Killer Strikes Again."

After Liberty and Bierly fled in Orion's car, Greytak shucked his bonds and called police. Orange County cops spread a net for Liberty, figuring he was headed for his old stomping grounds. But Liberty was not bound for Orange County. He appeared at a motel in Colorado Springs, Colo., run by Rudolph Brenek and his wife Edna. With Bierly, who came from Eugene, Ore., and Liberty was footloose Glen A. Fawcett, 17, of Midland, Tex. At 11:30 p.m.,

June 6, some 20 minutes after they checked in, the three came back to the office and with a .32 revolver took $109 in cash, a rifle and a credit card.

Unhappy with the take, they bound Edna and daughter Betty Rose while they ransacked the place. Unaccountably, they did not tie up Brenek. When they went to search the adjoining house, Brenek ducked out and phoned police.

By the time Brenek returned to the office, the bandits had fled, taking his wife as hostage.

Within moments, detectives Bernard Carter and Neal Stratton arrived at the motel. While Stratton checked out the license number of Liberty's car, Carter sped in pursuit. As Carter caught up, Liberty pegged six shots at him. At speeds of 100 mph the two cars roared through the Colorado night.

Now close, Carter saw Liberty fire again . . . and miss. Carter fired three warning shots. Fawcett drove on. As he drew near, Carter saw that Mrs. Brenek was in the backseat with Liberty, and he hesitated to fire for fear Liberty would kill her. Then Carter reasoned that if Liberty was going to kill the woman, he would do it whether Carter was there or not.

The lawman fired three shots into the fleeing auto; this took the fight out of Liberty. He threw his pistol out, stopped and gave up.

Charged with kidnapping, assault on a cop, robbery and auto theft, Liberty and Bierly pleaded innocent by reason of insanity and were ordered to the state hospital in Pueblo for psychiatric examination.

While in stir, the two married. Eventually, the Candlelight Killer was extradited to California for the Astorina-Orion murders. Judge Gardner caught heavy fire for freeing Liberty—to kill again and again. Ironically, Gardner was considered a tough judge. "I'll take the rap, but there is nothing I could do under the law but free him," Gardner declared.

In a San Diego jail, on Jan. 20, 1971, five days before he was to be put on trial for the bludgeon slaying of Orion, Liberty was strangled with his own shirt by his two cellmates, who believed, wrongly, that he was an informer for police.

The Candlelight Killer met the same senseless fate he had inflicted on others.

Who said Justice was blind?

When Justice Triumphed

This story appeared in the Daily News *on Jan. 6, 1924, and was the first "Justice Story" involving a solved crime. It carried no byline and took the overline, "When Justice Triumphed." For the first eight months of the "Justice" series, since the Joe Elwell murder mystery story of May 6, 1923, the cases had been unsolved and they bore the overline, "What Has Happened to Justice?"*

Thereafter, both overlines were used, as appropriate. At a much later date, they were dropped in favor of a logo, "The Justice Story."

I llicit love, an innocent teen child in search of her first job, a little gold-seal ring, a few strands of hair and a heap of blackened bones in a newly painted fireplace—these figured in the murder of Ruth Wheeler, one of the most gruesome crimes of the early 1900s and one of the most sensational. But above all, it was one of the most skillfully probed, for the body of the girl victim was built up again from a charred heap of bones so that even the exacting law was satisfied of her identity.

The scene of this story is the Yorkville of 1910, the clannish German colony of the East 70s and 80s, the Yorkville of the foaming Pilsener. Danger and crime seemed far removed from this bit of transplanted and happy Germany.

Yet there exited an unsavory little ménage of two persons—Katchen Muller and Albert Wolter. They lived together without benefit of clergy.

Katchen slaved 12 hours a day in a Third Avenue bakery. The youth was ostensibly looking for work after trying her hand at eight desultory jobs. Most of the time she loafed around Central Park. Note the spot! Central Park is just about the hardest place in New York in which to establish an alibi.

Both Katchen and Albert were immigrants and the children of immigrants. Neither was more than 18. They had met at a dance hall. Soon afterward Albert left his parents' home and they set up housekeeping at 224 E. 75th St.—a sordid home of which Katchen was the breadwinner. They talked vaguely of getting married when they should both come of age.

Now the scene shifts to the Merchants and Bankers Business College of that day. Into that college hopefully one morning there walked Ruth Amos Wheeler, one of its recent graduates, in search of a job. It was a Thursday, the 24th of March, 1910.

Ruth was 15, refined and pretty. A well-developed girl, she looked several years older than her age, but she was nevertheless the pet, the baby, of a family consisting of a widowed mother and three daughters. Her one ambition in life was to become a wage earner so that she might contribute her share to the family treasury. On that fateful Thursday she was looking for her first job.

A postcard had come into the college that morning saying that Albert Wolter of 224 E. 75th St. wanted a stenographer. Albert was neither a merchant nor a banker and he had about as much legitimate use for a stenographer as Central Park's zoological cow would have. But the school didn't investigate and Ruth didn't know.

When the postcard was handed to her, she took it gladly and went with hopeful tremors to the address given.

She rang the bell. Mrs. John Mohl, the landlady, heard it echoing through the building. The door to Wolter's apartment was opened by someone.

It closed and Ruth Wheeler never was seen alive again.

When Ruth did not come home to lunch, her mother thought merely that she had secured the coveted job. When she did not come home for dinner, the family was thoroughly alarmed. Pearl, an older sister of 28, called up the school and learned where Ruth had gone. Then she, too, rang the bell of the Seventy-fifth street address. Katchen came to the door, scantily dressed. Albert was already in bed. He sulkily insisted he knew nothing of the little sister.

Pearl looked in corners and closets. "Ruth," she called, "answer me if you're here, dear, and I'll help you."

Dead silence. She looked under the bed, and Albert, leering at her, made an insulting gesture. Terrified, she turned to the door, but the lock proved difficult to open.

"If you don't let me go, there's a policeman outside who will make you," she cried, bluffing it out with all the courage she possessed.

Katchen, wondering, opened the door, and the Wheeler girl fled to the nearest police station.

Katchen had wondered once before that day when she came home to find the iron screen removed from the grate and the fireplace daubed with bright green paint. They were short of money—it was her money, too—and she remonstrated with Albert.

"It was only 10 cents," he replied, adding that he had wanted to fix the place up for summer. It was only March then, but Katchen said nothing. However, in the night the disarranged screen tumbled down twice with a loud clang, waking her up each time. Albert refused to let her touch it, and insisted on getting up himself to fix it. Katchen, the sturdy breadwinner, was amazed at his solicitude.

The next evening, when she came home from her 12-hour grind, a detective awaited her. He followed her as she left the house again, saw her meet Albert, and trailed the two to a new home at 122 East 105th Street. There he arrested the lad for abducting Ruth Wheeler.

Back at the 75th Street house, all went as before. The departure of Albert and Katchen caused not a ripple in the daily lives of those humble people. Even a day or so later when Mrs. John Taggart, in the next apartment, saw a bulky sack on the fire escape, which passed both her windows and those of Wolter and Katchen's late apartment, she thought it was only the shiftlessness of "those two," and she asked her husband to take it away. Taggart, tired from his day's work, kicked the bundle from the fire escape down into the courtyard below. When it was still there March 26, he went downstairs and poked around in the bag.

To his utter amazement, he found in that ghastly sack the burned torso and arms of a woman, with a finely woven rope around the neck. He dashed to the nearest police station.

Then began one of the most searching pieces of detective work in the annals of modern crime. Not only was it searching but it was complete, for the body was defaced beyond recognition. Yet Ruth Wheeler was identified to the satisfaction of the law from those charred bones and bit by bit was built up a complete and convincing case against that stolid, brutish German youth of 18.

In a short time the old and new homes of Wolter and Katchen were being thoroughly ransacked. Behind the screen in the newly painted fireplace were found equally hideous evidences of crime—blackened bones; a left hand tightly clenched about a few hairs; bits of clothing; stains of blood. Amid these relics were a hatpin belonging to Ruth Wheeler and a signet ring with the initial "R.A.W." The missing girl's umbrella was discovered in a closet at the 105th Street address.

The day after that—and the days now are certain—the German youth was discharged on the abduction charge and rearrested for murder. Stolidly he maintained that he knew nothing of the girl. He had not been at home that day. After breakfast, he had purchased paint for the fireplace; then he had looked for work and ended up in Central Park. He lunched at Katchen's bakery and then went back to the park, returning home about 3:00.

"Seems to me you spent a lot of time in Central Park," snapped Capt. Carey of the Homicide Squad, in charge of the investigation.

Wolter stuck to his guns. Katchen was arrested and told police of the green paint and the fire screen tumbling down in the night. Wolter's father said the boy was no good, could never hold a job, and had been cast off by his parents because of his shiftlessness.

Most incriminating of all, in Wolter's notebook, was found the sentence: "Ruth Amos Wheeler, age fifteen, American, lives with parents, wages $7."

Evidence piled on evidence—circumstantial but damning. When Taggart found the bag, it had been tied up with picture wire, and Wolter's truck yielded a coil of the same wire.

Thirty-six hours of grilling failed to shake the youth's denial. Pale, with twitching fingers, but with a stolid front, he replied to the questions of the police. Then suddenly he wilted, wept, groveled on the floor and promised to tell all. The reason for this astonishing change of front was a letter from his Katchen saying she loved him in spite of everything. As soon as he learned that she had forgiven him, Wolter answered his questioners. He would tell the whole truth. He begged for a night's rest.

And after that night's rest, the dim and wraithlike figure of Frederick Ahner made its appearance in the case.

At first, he was simply a friend, an ex-waiter and expert stenographer. The two were going to start a shorthand school for girls out of work, narrated Wolter, the friend teaching shorthand, and Wolter German. They answered newspaper advertisements of girls who wanted jobs. The friend had access to his rooms, Wolter insisted, and "if Miss Wheeler did go to the flat and meet anyone, she must have met his friend, for I was not in the house at the time."

An amazing story in the face of those relics in the fireplace, the new green paint, the dislodged screen clattering to the floor in the night, the sentence in the notebook! As amazing as the crime itself, in its stupidity.

Meanwhile, coroner's physician O'Hanlon had been going over the mortal remains of what had once been Ruth Wheeler. Death, he found, was due to "strangulation and incineration," but he found more than that. Ruth had been burned to death while *still alive*, and before the murder, an even more fiendish crime had been perpetrated upon her.

"Murder" was the verdict of the coroner's jury. And here, again, the German lad showed another of his astounding evidences of insensibility. With the finger of justice pointing directly at him, his chief expostulation was—that he didn't want to face the crowd in the coroner's courtroom without a *collar*.

Within two days, Wolter had been indicted for homicide by the grand jury and had been arraigned, pleading, "Not guilty" in a shout that astonished even the hardened attendants of the Supreme Court. On April 18, 1910, he was put on trial for murder.

While he was waiting in jail, Wolter missed the girl who had provided him with bread and butter. He pleaded with officers of the law to be allowed to marry his Katchen. They refused. For Katchen was to testify against him, and a woman cannot be forced to testify against her husband.

All this time, with Wolter in the Tombs, facing a murder trial, with Katchen in the House of Detention, where was "Frederick Ahner," if there were indeed any such person? Wolter soon sought to prove the existence of this spook. He produced a letter "From-the-Man-Who-Ought-to-be-in-Prison-in-Your-Place," which declared that the writer would come forward at the proper moment to save his substitute from the electric chair.

The Wolter trial was to 1910 a matter of sensational interest. As usual, well-dressed women thronged the courtroom and fought to get in after the chamber was filled. As usual, sob sisters and newspaper artists were there to augment the usual throng of reporters, all with their eyes trained on Wolter, the odd-featured youth with the weak, womanish mouth, the violet eyes, the neatly brushed light brown hair, and the ears like fans.

The courtroom was a veritable morgue. All the gruesome relics of Ruth Wheeler's passing were there.

From those charred bones, Ruth Wheeler had risen as effectively as though she had come back in the flesh to demand vengeance. There was no doubt in the mind of anybody that the body was that of Ruth, but the law demands unassailable proof of the identification.

And so the prosecution had reconstructed Ruth's body from the debris, pieced together the body, section by section, measured her height, judged her weight, noted the clenched bones of the left hand and proved not only that the body was Ruth's, but that she had been murdered in the most brutal fashion.

That prosecution proved once and for all that, with ingenuity and determination, Justice can claim its own.

Prof. George S. Huntington of Columbia University, famous anatomist, appeared at the trial, ready to do the whole thing over again if the court deemed it necessary as evidence.

The morbid crowd of spectators held its breath until lawyer Schott waived his right to this particular demonstration. The professor produced the left hand.

Embedded between the small bones were a gold signet ring with the initials "R.A.W." and a few strands of yellowish brown hair when the hand was found, he testified.

Yellowish brown hair. Ruth's hair had been reddish brown. The hair of the prisoner was yellowish brown.

"I object," shouted attorney Scott.

Assistant District Attorney Frank Moss, the prosecutor, let it go. But he had the professor repeat the statement that the hair in the girl's hand had been yellowish brown, quite different from the color of her own hair, as testified to by her mother and sisters.

That little ring was for Wolter what the noose around her neck had been to his victim. Without it, identification had been incomplete. But the ring! Pearl testified weeping that she had given it to her little sister for Christmas, and that ring and those hairs sent Wolter to the electric chair.

Ruth's mother, a simple, hardworking woman, identified the remains of her daughter with forced calm. "Yes, that looks to me like Ruth's—my little girl's hair."

Pearl, quiet and straightforward, told of her visit to Wolter's apartment on the day of her sister's disappearance. Adelaide Wheeler, 19, Ruth's other sister, told of the clothes Ruth had worn that morning. A Second Avenue merchant testified to Wolter's having purchased kerosene from him the morning of the murder, shattering the Central Park alibi. A clerk in a 10-cent store on Third Avenue told of Wolter having bought the paint that same morning, giving another blow to the alibi. A woman who kept a cigar and stationery store across the street said she had seen him in the doorway of his house that morning.

Never did a man go on trial for his life on circumstantial evidence with a more complete case against him. Owing to the skillful work of Capt. Carey and his detectives, Wolter was faced on every hand with incriminating evidence. Not the smallest point, not the most insignificant person had been ignored.

With stolid assurance, Wolter told again the incredible story of Frederick Ahner. This other man was a young German and a waiter at Coney Island, he said. They had become acquainted and had planned to start a shorthand school. Later Ahner became his evil genius. It was Ahner who sent the postcard to the business school. It was he who dictated the entry in Wolter's memorandum book. He had disappeared now, but he would come back at the proper time.

Ahner never came, and Judge Warren W. Foster did not believe in Ahner's existence anyhow. Neither did the jury. They considered the verdict three hours and 33 minutes, and two of the hours were spent eating dinner. Their verdict was first-degree murder, and Wolter was sentenced to die the week of June 6. That same day, he went to Sing Sing, where he stayed for 676 days while his appeal was slowly considered and digested by the higher court.

At 5:38 a.m. on Jan. 29, 1912, Wolter went through the little green door to his death stolidly, with the ghost of Frederick Ahner still on his lips and a prayer that "God may bring the guilty one to justice." But Justice was quite satisfied with the penalty paid by Albert Wolter, who at least did exist.

The scene shifts once more. It is years later in Yorkville. Katchen, the ashy-haired, red-handed servant girl, is disproving the story that it is the woman who pays and pays and pays. Katchen is happily married to a sturdy young German who knows her past and loves her in spite of it.

The Courtesan of Broadway

JOSEPH MCNAMARA
APRIL 13, 1986

G ray-eyed and red-haired Vivian Gordon would have captured attention in any era. But on the morning of Feb. 26, 1931— wearing a Parisian black velvet dress, chic cocktail hat, silk undies, sheer stockings and one black suede pump—she commanded the attention of all New Yorkers, for she also wore a six-foot length of dirty clothesline tightened fatally around her pretty neck.

Vivian, at 38, still shapely enough to warrant her title of the Courtesan of Broadway, was that very morning slated to appear before the Seabury Committee probing corruption in the police department of Mayor Jimmy "Beau James" Walker.

Gordon had charged that an undercover vice detective had framed her in a prostitution arrest, and the committee, headed by

Judge Samuel Seabury, wanted proof. There were some New Yorkers cynical enough after weeks of aired police corruption to believe vice squad detectives had taken Vivian for a ride.

In any event, she turned up dead in a ravine near the Mosholu Parkway entrance to Van Cortlandt Park in the Bronx. An autopsy indicated she had eaten a substantial meal and consumed a goodly amount of whiskey. There was no evidence of rape.

Missing from the body were Vivian's $665 diamond wristwatch, $2,000 diamond ring and $1,800 mink coat that an elevator man reported she was wearing when she left her luxury apartment on E. 37th St. at 11:30 the night before. Police immediately concluded the ex-actress and former chorine had been slain by robbers.

Then it was learned that, 19 days before, she had written the Seabury Committee that Detective Andrew McLaughlin had connived with her former husband, John Bischoff, to arrest her for prostitution in 1923. During her stretch in Bedford Reformatory, Bischoff got custody of their seven-year-old daughter, Benita.

As Vivian retold it, she was a broke film extra and sometime model when she encountered McLaughlin in a car while on her way home.

"I told him my hard-luck story and he said he would help out," she said. "He put $20 in my stocking."

Gordon took him to a friend's apartment, where McLaughlin announced the arrest.

As headlines blared the murder mystery, Judge Seabury addressed Police Commissioner Edward P. Mulrooney: "May I ask you to apprise me of the circumstances surrounding the death of Vivian Gordon?"

Mulrooney blew his stack. "Vivian Gordon was an expert racketeer!" he exclaimed. "When she supplied pretty women for parties, she instructed them to find out the names, social positions and financial standings of the men."

After which Vivian would blackmail them, the commissioner said. In Gordon's apartment, sleuths found a racy diary with an ample supply of possible suspects and a book listing 40 party girls and the names of 560 prominent men—blackmail victims or prospective ones, Mulrooney said.

"Until this case is cleared up, every policeman in New York has a smudge on his shield!" thundered Mulrooney.

For 134 days the boys in blue sought to prove the killer was a blackmail victim or a thief. They checked out blackmail victims clear across the country and dug into Gordon's background.

She was born Benita Franklin, daughter of the warden of Joliet Prison in Illinois, and was convent-reared in Canada. Moody and insubordinate, she ran away at 18 and toured with humdrum theatrical companies.

After marrying Bischoff and, in 1921, dumping him in Philadelphia, Vivian came to New York with her daughter and reportedly worked the streets until McLaughlin made his collar. Out of stir, she decided to let others do the work and got some girls and a few steerers.

Now she was dead.

McLaughlin and Bischoff headed the list of suspects. The ex-hubby came to New York and told cops his divorce was based on cruelty, that he never mentioned vice. He did not know McLaughlin, Bischoff said.

A six-day cruise to Bermuda at the time of the murder was the effective alibi of McLaughlin, but he came to grief with Seabury, who wanted to know how he banked $35,800 in two years on a salary of $3,000 annually. McLaughlin refused to divulge his financial savvy. He was fired.

Other names came out of the diary. There was John Radeloff, Vivian's attorney, financial advisor and one-time lover. When Radeloff moved out on the sex doll, she threatened to tell his wife, and he, in turn, vowed to have her bumped off by Sam "Chowderhead" Cohen, a rotund ex-safecracker and former bodyguard of Vivian's. But both Radeloff and Cohen had tight alibis.

Another diary entry mentioned a $1,500 loan to a Charles Reuben. After his name were the letters OSLO.

Probers checked Scandinavian steamships for the time of the entry and found Reuben booked aboard the Berengaria. He was in a stateroom with a James Cotter and Sam Cohen. Chowderhead quickly proved he was not "that" Sam Cohen. Examination of Reuben's handwriting by a graphologist indicated the writing was that of Harry Stein, who did six years in Sing Sing for trying to strangle a Bronx woman. Vivian was strangled in the Bronx.

Now, it seems, Stein was a close friend of Gordon's. He was put under constant surveillance, as were two friends, Harry Greenberg and Harry Harvey. The two Harrys were seen passing money and the probe intensified. It now turned out the "Sam Cohen" on the cruise was actually Greenberg. And "Cotter" was "Harry Harvey," who really was Harry Schlitten.

Probers learned that within an hour of Vivian's murder, Stein approached a "fence" with a fur coat, diamond ring and wristwatch identical to the slain woman's. Mulrooney sized up Schlitten as the weak one and urged his detectives to break him. He broke—and led detectives to a spot where Vivian's other suede pump had been tossed from the car. The shoe was found.

On May 25 Mulrooney announced a confession from Schlitten that went this way:

Stein, discussing Vivian's blackmail racket, told Schlitten, "If I don't put a certain party out of the way, a friend of mine is going to wind up in jail."

The night of Feb. 25, Schlitten and Greenberg picked up Stein in a rented car. Stein had a rope and said, "We'll get $1,000 to $2,000 out of this tonight."

Stein was dropped at Vivian's apartment while Schlitten drove Greenberg to Grand Avenue, Bronx. Greenberg's only knowledge of the affair was that he was supposed to be a patsy with $250,000 in uncut stones that Stein was busy convincing Vivian she could cajole out of him with a few wiles.

Soon Stein and Vivian arrived in a taxi and got into the backseat of the rented auto with Greenberg. As she was introduced to Greenberg, Vivian cooed, "Where have you been all my life?"

Schlitten, at the wheel, said he heard a scuffle as Stein applied the rope.

"She only cackled once," Schlitten declared.

In late June, Stein and Greenberg were tried before Bronx Supreme Court justice Albert Cohn. Schlitten testified that the day after the murder, Stein sold Vivian's ring for $600 and gave him $212. The money exchanged by the "Harrys" was part of the loot, Schlitten related.

Defense attorney Samuel Leibowitz tore into Schlitten and got him to admit the DA had promised him immunity for his testimony. Stein and Greenberg offered alibis—and the jury believed them. A gasp went up in court at the not-guilty verdict.

An assistant DA called it "the gravest miscarriage of justice ever in the Bronx." Crowed Leibowitz: "A case tailor-made by the police will never hold water before a jury of 12 sensible men."

No one was ever convicted of Vivian Gordon's murder. But police insisted the case was solved, the jury simply did not believe it. As for justice, it prevailed but was delayed, lawmen said. On July 9, 1955, Stein died in Sing Sing's electric chair for the $1,200 stickup-murder of a *Reader's Digest* messenger in 1950.

This Mummy's Boy Was a Head-hunting Hobbyist

JOSEPH MCNAMARA
JULY 26, 1987

Ed Gein never cursed, smoked or drank. His mother would not have liked it. Ed did have some vices his ma would not have approved of, though, like murdering several women and looting the graves of a dozen more. But by that time his ma had passed on to wherever stern, dominating women go after death.

Gein had other good qualities. He was a soft-spoken handyman who worked hard and never overcharged for his efforts. He never lied. The kind folk of Plainfield, Wis., entrusted their babysitting chores to good old Ed. If it just wasn't for that business of killing, and the graves. . . .

That's why when Ed Gein told his chilling story in 1957, the people in Wisconsin's scenic lake region of Waushura County were shocked. The macabre details caught the eye of author Robert Block, whose book about Ed caught the eye of Alfred Hitchcock, whose film *Psycho* caught the eye of just about everyone.

Ed had been brought to a run-down 195-acre farm seven miles from Plainfield in 1914 when he was a scrawny seven-year-old. He lived with his mother Augusta, father George and an older brother, Henry. The Geins were not so friendly with the people of Plainfield, a village of 680 souls 125 miles northwest of Milwaukee.

Ma ruled her roost in stiff sateen dresses she herself made to hide every womanly curve. She drew her straight, lusterless hair tightly across her scalp and fastened it in a prim chignon in back.

Men, Ma warned Ed, were not of much account, but women were the emissaries of the devil. Augusta apparently exempted herself. At least, Ed thought so. He worshipped his mother. No dating for Ed.

In the early 1940s, Ed's father died, then brother Henry . . . and Ma was left with her favorite son. In 1945 she suffered a stroke. Ed refused nursing care and tended to her himself. When she died, he converted her room into a shrine.

There was another woman in Gein's life, Adeline Watkins, 40ish, a spinster who wore horn-rimmed glasses, her hair in bangs. They usually got together at her home, never his, which was incredibly cluttered. When they went out, Ed had her back by 10 p.m., as her mother urged.

They spoke of books and lions and murder stories, and Ed told her about his mother, interminably, and of his hobby of collecting shrunken heads. He knew much about anatomy and embalming, Watkins realized. His last date with her was Feb. 6, 1955.

"That night, he proposed," Adeline said later. "Not in so many words, but I knew what he meant. He was kind and sweet but I turned him down. . . . I was afraid I wouldn't be able to live up to what he expected of me."

Watkins was shrewd enough to realize Ed had confronted her with an unattainable ideal of womanhood—his mother. That was the end of dating for Ed.

Gein renewed his shrunken head hobby, and in the fall of 1957 things came to a climax. On Nov. 16, he drove to the hardware store run by widow Bernice Worden, 58, and her son, Frank. The son was off hunting. Ed bought a can of antifreeze and Worden duly noted the sale in her journal.

A later customer found Mrs. Worden missing, along with her truck. There was a splatter of blood at the store. Sheriff Arthur Schley found Fein's name the last item in Worden's sales book, and he and his deputies raced to the Gein farm. They found no sign of Gein. They did find, in a kitchen, the body of Worden, stripped and decapitated, hung by the heels from a rafter.

Sickened with shock, the lawmen searched further. They found 10 female "masks," fashioned from actual faces gleaned from ghoulish nighttime visits Gein made to the cemetery. It was later established that Gein had lopped the tops off the heads, hollowed out the insides and embalmed them and saved them in plastic bags. These were undoubtedly Gein's collection of "shrunken heads."

Five of the masks were placed at eye level, so Ed could stand and talk to them, lawmen believed.

Sheriff Hebert Wansersky of Portage County came over to help, and he recognized one of the masks as the face of Mrs. Mary Hogan, 54, who three years before had vanished from the rural bar she operated some six miles from Gein's farm.

Gein was arrested at the home of a neighbor, where he usually took his nighttime meal. He was given two days of lie detector tests, after which Gein confessed to killing Hogan. Oddly, he said he did not remember slaying Worden. But her butchered remains in his summer kitchen told officers all they needed to know. They believed Gein shot Worden in the store.

Most of the heads, Ed insisted, came from the graves. But this did little to allay the nausea that affected those in the village.

More horrors were revealed. Deputies reported finding in Ed's home four chairs upholstered with human skin. A drum was made from the same. Could this be the work of slim, little Ed Gein, the innocuous handyman, the village baby-sitter? Headlines now proclaimed him "The Butcher of Plainfield" and "Ghoul Gein."

Psychiatrists said that Gein, strongly attached to his domineering mother, eventually desired to be a woman himself. He even considered self-surgery but gave up that idea. The masks which he donned at home and the other female paraphernalia enabled him to find satisfaction in this ghastly charade, they said.

One doctor said he killed the women because they resembled his dead mother.

Gein was charged with Worden's murder. Examined by psychiatrists, Ed was found incompetent to stand trial by Circuit Judge Herbert Bunde, who on Jan. 6, 1958, ordered him committed to Central State Hospital in Waupun.

Judge Bunde expressed confidence that Gein would never again see the outside world. But in 1967 the village was jolted by the news that Ed Gein had been declared competent to stand trial.

Gein was convicted of first-degree murder, but was declared innocent by reason of insanity and landed back in the same hospital. Over the years, Ed did great carpentry and masonry work in Central State, but he reached a point when he wanted out.

In June 1974, Gein bid for his freedom in a hearing before Circuit Judge Robert Gollman. Now stooped and gray, Gein said he had recovered his sanity and was unhappy at the hospital.

Prosecutor Robert Rudolph protested that Gein had not recovered his sanity, that he was still a danger to others and to himself. Four psychiatrists agreed. Judge Gollman ruled that Gein was still mentally ill and should remain at Central State.

"Besides, people might not treat him very well," the judge noted. "Some people might even try to exhibit him," he added sadly.

On July 26, 1984, Ed Gein, suffering from cancer, died at Central State of respiratory failure. He was 77. In Spiritland Cemetery, Ed Gein was buried in an unmarked grave next to the mother whose death had left him adrift in a strange world.

His Wife Made Him Boiling Mad

JOSEPH MCNAMARA
SEPTEMBER 21, 1986

A dolph Louis Luetgert was a man of gargantuan appetites, not the least of which was a dedicated, lustful pursuit of the ladies. But most Chicagoans of the Gay Nineties knew him simply as the best maker of German sausage in the city. He was soon to grab national headlines in another matter.

Luetgert had not come to his talent of palate-teasing easily. He had wooed several other trades, including farming and tanning, in the Chicago area before making it big with his spiced meat products. Born in Germany in 1848, Luetgert had come to America in the 1870s and settled in the Windy City with its large German population.

Having chosen the sausage business, Adolph toiled long and hard in the sweaty chase of success—which came with time. Luetgert was a cask of a man, 6-feet-3 with tremendous girth, as befits one who appreciated a groaning table and tankards of beer and ale. He had brown eyes and brown hair.

As he built up his sausage business, his first wife died and left him with one child. In the 1880s Luetgert married Louisa Bicknese, whose bulk aped his own. Just why he married Louisa was never clear to confidants, since he complained about her from day one.

However, Louisa apparently occupied a small part of Luetgert's schedule. Much of his day was spent at the sausage works, and the remainder of his time had to be divided among his three constant mistresses plus any other woman he could clutch to his 250-pound frame.

To make this pleasant task easier, Luetgert had installed a massive bed at his sausage factory—well beyond the prying eyes of Louisa.

Among his steady sex partners was Louisa's maid, Mary Simering. Then there was the wealthy Christine Feldt. The trio was rounded out by Agatha Tosch, who with her husband operated a gin mill on the north side of Chicago, not far from the factory, located at Diversey and Hermitage Sts.

Luetgert's factory ground out huge amounts of sausage, but his costs rose disproportionately higher. And with the amorous demands Luetgert had put upon himself, he found little time to cope with the problem. Then, instead of trying to cut costs, he decided to get more capital and enlarge the business. By early 1897, it was obvious this plan was a failure.

To ease the mental anguish, Luetgert lost himself in extramarital sexploits that even his placid wife could no longer ignore. Indignantly, she accosted Luetgert, who, in a rage, began to choke her. Only the last-minute realization that horrified neighbors were looking in the parlor windows prompted the wanton hubby to release his wife.

But that was not the end of it. A few days later, neighbors were subjected to the sight of the portly sensualist chasing Louisa down the street, waving a revolver at her.

While the harried wife survived these assaults, a deadly plan was unfolding in Luetgert's fevered mind, according to later police investigations. The law made these points:

On March 11, 1897, the sausage-maker ordered 325 pounds of crude potash and 50 pounds of arsenic from a wholesale firm, and it was delivered to his factory the next day.

On April 24, Luetgert told an employee, "Smokehouse Frank" Odorowsky, to move the potash to the basement of the factory, where three huge vats were used to boil sausage meat. The potash, at Luetgert's direction, was put into the middle vat and the steam turned on. The powder turned into liquid.

On May 1, Luetgert told his night watchman, Frank Bialk, to buy him a bottle of celery water at a nearby drugstore, and later that evening sent him out on another errand. On returning both times, Bialk found his boss locked in the basement room. Luetgert remained there until 2 a.m.

What he was doing there could not be guessed at until young Emma Schiemicke later told police that as she passed the factory at 10:30 that night with her sister, she saw Luetgert leading his wife up the alley behind the sausage works. Louisa was not seen again.

As police later reconstructed it, Bialk noticed the next day that there was a glue-like substance on the floor in front of the middle vat and laced through it what looked like bone flakes. But Bialk thought nothing of it, which speaks volumes about the content of Luetgert's sausages.

The next day, Smokehouse Frank saw the same gooey mess and mentioned it to his boss.

"Don't say anything about it, and I'll see that you have a good job for life," Luetgert assertedly told him.

When Louisa's brother, Diedrich Bicknese, called on her the next day, Luetgert told him she had left the house May 1 and never returned. Asked why he had not reported it to police, Luetgert said he wanted to avoid any scandal.

The brother went to the cops, and a captain who knew of the Luetgerts' dustups asked why the butcher had worried him about a missing dog but did not report his wife missing.

The bulky husband said he expected his wife to return, and again mentioned his fear of scandal.

Questioning of Bialk and Smokehouse Frank on May 7 soon brought the captain around to the middle vat, three-quarters full of a strange liquid.

He ordered it strained through burlap. Found were some bones that Luetgert insisted were animal remains, although medicos labeled them human.

Also discovered were two lady's gold rings, one inscribed with the initials L.L. Luetgert did not explain these.

Relatives identified the rings as Louisa's and told authorities she could not remove them because of swollen finger joints.

The sausage-maker was charged with boiling her right out of her rings.

Luetgert's trial was sensational. The defense argued that the bones were animal waste Luetgert was boiling down with potash to make soft soap to clean his factory.

Ridiculous, countered the prosecution. Why would he spend $40 to make soft soap he could buy for $1?

His three mistresses testified against him. Tosch said that when she asked him where his wife was, he replied in agitation, "I'm innocent as the southern skies." She said the butcher claimed to have hated his wife and once told her, "I could just crush her."

Feldt, whom Luetgert considered his one true love, revealed the hulk's boyishly smitten letters to her. Even more telling, she said the day after Louisa had vanished, Luetgert gave her a bloodstained knife, which she produced for the court.

Another witness swore that the defendant had told her that if it were not for the maid, Mary Simering, he "would not stay at home."

On Feb. 9, 1898, the German immigrant was convicted of stabbing his wife and rendering her to liquid in the sausage vat.

He was sentenced to life in prison and hustled off to Joliet State Prison. There, in 1911, he gave up the ghost, protesting his innocence to the bitter end.

Police Nip Career of Mass Murderer at English Resort

PETER LEVINS
AUGUST 13, 1939

S hadrach Garrett, superintendent of police at Bournemouth, England, scribbled the bare details in his memorandum pad:

"Dec. 23, 1921. Dead woman 5 feet 4 inches in height, medium build, teeth prominent. Wore no rings or jewelry. Had heavy brown coat, purple woolen blouse, navy blue skirt and black shoes and stockings. Hat of dark brown suede with pink ribbon interlaced under the crown. Clothing showed several large rents. Must have been violent struggle. Splotches of blood all around the body. Had been badly battered from clubbing."

Garrett then resumed his examination at the scene, a field skirting the Seafield Road junction. He noticed that a gold watch, pinned on the victim's left breast, bore the initials "I.W.W." And that a tag on an article of clothing carried the name "I.W. Wilkins."

The body was removed to Bournemouth, popular summer resort, where a postmortem revealed that Wilkins had not been criminally assaulted. Coroner's verdict—willful murder.

During the luncheon hour that same day, Noel Harry Wilkins, a London bank clerk, read the story and realized that the victim must be his sister, Irene. Friends accompanied him to Bournemouth where, white-faced and shaking, he made the identification.

Wilkins told Garrett that his unmarried sister had been an inspector of army canteens in a factory at Gretna Green during the war. Since then, she usually worked as a cook—recently she had told him that she intended to advertise for a job. This led to a check of newspaper files and discovery of the following advertisement in the *Morning Post* of Dec. 22:

"Lady cook (31) requires post in school; experienced in school with 40 boarders: disengaged; salary—I. Wilkins, 21 Thirlmere Road, London, S.W."

Wilkins said that at 11:45 that morning his sister received a telegram via the Boscombe office. This read:

"Wilkins, 21 Thirlmere Road, London, S.W., Morning Post. Come immediately, 4:30 train, Waterloo, Bournemouth Central.

Car will meet train. Expense no object. Urgent—Wood Beech House."

Naturally delighted at the quick response to her ad, Miss Wilkins had left her home at 3 that afternoon, taking an overnight bag and a few toilet articles.

That was the extent of the clues with which Garrett had to work at the outset of the investigation. He, incidentally, was not a detective at all; he had spent all his official life as an officer of the Hants County Constabulary and had finally been promoted to the superintendency at Bournemouth. He was used to the quiet life of a highly respectable summer resort with austere boarding house residents. A murder to him was something entirely new.

But that did not mean he did not know his business.

His first move, after seeing that the newspapers had a description of the victim, was to invite all persons who might have information to communicate with him. Within a few days he received 22,000 communications. Some merely gave suggestions, others thought they had known Miss Wilkins, a few were really helpful.

One caller at Garrett's office was a Bournemouth taxicab driver who reported that he had seen a young woman resembling Miss Wilkins alight from the train on the afternoon of the 22nd. He said she was met by a man dressed as a chauffeur, and they had driven away in a well-appointed car.

The number of the license plate was partly hidden, the informant said.

Another chauffeur, a driver for the Royal Bath Hotel bus, remembered seeing a young woman of Miss Wilkins' description immediately after she got off the train. He had asked her if she wanted a taxi and she had replied, "No, thank you; a car is coming to pick me up."

Then he, too, had seen a private car arrive and go off with the visitor. He described the chauffeur of this car as about 30 years old, clean-shaven, dark, square-jawed, and rather illiterate in speech. He was wearing a chauffeur's uniform.

Superintendent Garrett, with this information at hand, tried to reconstruct the murder in his own mind. The private car had left the Bournemouth station at 7:15 p.m., then proceeded by a lonely back road to a lonely spot at Tuckton, where two roads divide, forming the junction. There, Miss Wilkins had, apparently, been dragged from the car, beaten to death with a heavy screw hammer, then tossed into the bushes.

Now, the case took a sudden, strange turn.

A nurse named Martha Burnside, also of London, reported that she had inserted an advertisement in the previous issue of the *Post*—and had received a telegram from Bournemouth, signed, "Mrs. Cooper." She had followed instructions, but no one had met her at the station, so she had returned to London.

But this was not all. A Norwegian girl, Betty Ditmausen, said she had advertised and also received a telegram worded the same as the nurse Burnside summons. She had not answered the wire because she considered Bournemouth too far away to suit her. The telegram read:

"Boscombe. Re advertisement. Immediate interview required. Take 4:30 Waterloo Bournemouth Central. Expenses paid if required. Stay overnight. Car will meet you, Mrs. Cooper."

Investigation developed that, in the original copy of the telegram to Miss Ditmausen, the word "advertisement" had been spelled "advertisment," and the word "if" had been spelled with a double "f." Also, "expenses paid" had been written "expences paye."

It appeared that the suspect had not confined his messages merely to persons who had advertised in the newspapers, for the police learned that, two days before the murder, he had wired a West End employment agency as follows:

"Cavendish Bureau, 12 Princess Street, London, W.E. Please send by 5:30 Waterloo to Boscombe young pleasant nurse companion for girl 20. Car will meet train. About ten days. Urgent—Butler, Boscombe Grange."

That the same man had written the Wilkins, Burnside and Ditmausen messages was indicated by the handwriting of the originals. And he had made the same mistakes in spelling. (The telegram to the Cavendish agency had been dictated over the phone.)

The next person to shed light on the mystery was Lillian Diplock, a clerk at the Boscombe post office. She told Garrett that on Dec. 22, at 10:15 a.m., a telegram to Miss Wilkins was handed in by a man who answered the description of the suspect. She said he was 5 feet 6 or 7, about 30, dark-complexioned, and was dressed as a chauffeur.

The clerk recalled that the same man had sent telegrams to Miss Burnside and Miss Ditmausen.

In addition to containing the same errors in spelling, each message offered conclusive evidence in the fact that the word "come" was written in the same peculiar fashion in each. The letter "m" had a big loop, and was formed very curiously—it would hardly have been imitated or repeated except by the person whose natural handwriting it was.

Garrett, acting on the theory that the suspect lived in Bournemouth, now undertook the task of searching for handwriting that resembled the scrawl on the telegrams. His men started with local hotel registers and boarding houses, but found nothing to speed the search for the killer.

Meanwhile, all ports were watched. The description of the suspect was broadcast—age 28 to 30; 5 feet 6 to 5 feet 8; dressed in chauffeur's hat and overcoat, blue in color; having the appearance of a chauffeur; uneducated of speech. Probably used employer's car.

On Jan. 1, 12 days after the body was found, Benjamin Barnby, a groom, was walking through the woods at Bournemouth when he came upon an overnight bag lying open with various articles scattered about. He notified Garrett, who found in addition a small bag containing a comb and brush, a toothbrush, nightgown and other necessities. Also the telegram requesting Wilkins to come to Bournemouth.

The killer, it appeared, had gone through the overnight bag rather hurriedly and had not bothered to destroy the telegram.

This discovery did not bring the police any nearer to the identity of the slayer, but it did establish one important fact—the direction in which he drove from the scene of the crime. It also supplied presumptive evidence that the suspect was either a local man or one who knew his way about the region.

The 60 chauffeurs who lived in or about Bournemouth were, naturally, closely examined. No evidence was found against any of them, but several were kept under surveillance. Among the latter was Thomas Henry Allaway of Boscombe.

Allaway, 36, a married man and a war veteran, worked for Arthur Warwick Sutton of Barton Close, Southborne, which is a short distance from the scene of the crime. His employer told Garrett that Allaway had worked for him more than a year and was a model private chauffeur.

The garage keeper said that the Sutton car, a 1914 gray four-seater Mercedes, had been locked up in the garage at 6 p.m., Dec. 22, and had not been taken out until the following day. This indicated that it could not have been in use at the time the murder took place. The garage man was the only person entrusted with the keys to the garage.

Allaway normally reported for work at 10:30 in the morning. From about 1:15 until 3 he would be free; and unless exceptional circumstances arose, he would be free after 5:30.

Superintendent Garrett, carefully checking on every aspect of the case, was interested to learn that, on Dec. 25, 26 and 27, the days when local chauffeurs and their cars were being examined, Thomas Henry Allaway took sick leave and did not report for work. Garrett was also interested to learn that Allaway had changed the style of parting his hair. Also that he was now wearing a slightly different uniform.

Now, the chief investigator had another visitor with information to contribute. Alice Frances Waters, a post office clerk, told him that, while she was stationed at Bournemouth, she had taken the telegram addressed to the employment agency. The incident had impressed itself on her mind because her sister had been trying to find such a position as the message stipulated.

Then, again, she recalled that the man's voice had not been quite clear. When she asked him to repeat, he had exclaimed impatiently, "Car—car will meet."

Subsequent to this, Waters continued, she was transferred to the Boscombe post office. In the course of her duties, she said, she was startled to hear the voice of a man who handed a parcel to one of her co-workers. (This was several days after the Wilkins murder.) It sounded very much like the voice of the man who sent the telegram.

Waters had confided her suspicions to other employees. Accordingly, the man's car had been followed as it drove away from the post office.

The driver turned out to be Allaway.

Garrett, still seeking evidence to justify an arrest, now turned his attention to a statement by Frank Humphries, a motor designer who had traveled on the same train as Wilkins. Humphries had noticed a car of unusual design at the Bournemouth station, and so had studied it with an appraising eye.

He told the authorities that his interest in the car, a Mercedes, had been so aroused that he had asked his son to take down the license number, in case he might wish to look up the manufacturer. The number was LK-7405—which was the number on the Sutton car.

This was the car which was supposed to have been locked up at the time of the murder.

Garrett decided to gather some of Allaway's handwriting before he sent the decoy telegrams. This was by no means easy. The suspect's home was searched, but yielded no samples. Then, the investigator visited the local taxation office, where he examined Allaway's application for a chauffeur's license.

The word "car" on the license bore a striking resemblance to the same word in the telegrams.

Now, Allaway began to break under pressure. Detectives trailing him watched him make some unlucky bets on horse races, then saw him cash several checks at local stores. It developed that he had stolen his employer's checkbook, and that the checks were forged.

Next, the suspect sent his wife and three-year-old daughter to the home of his in-laws in Reading. Then, assuming the name of Cook, he bolted for Kilburn, where he had formerly lived. Detectives traced him to Kilburn, but lost him there.

Garrett heard about these developments and was immensely pleased. He had not gathered enough evidence yet to warrant an arrest for murder, but now he could seize his man for forgery. Accordingly, he asked the police at Kilburn and at Reading to be on the lookout.

Hardly had the request been delivered when the Reading police had Allaway in custody.

Garrett still wanted to hurdle the obstacle presented by the fact that the Sutton car could not have been in the garage at the same time that it was at the Bournemouth station. He realized that if this difficulty was not solved, then Allaway might escape conviction—or even prosecution. The garage proprietor had continued to insist that the car had been locked up for the night well before Wilkins arrived at Bournemouth.

"Search every inch of the man's flat in Boscombe," the chief directed his men. "Allaway must have had a key. He must have taken the car because we know that he met the train in the Mercedes."

They searched the flat and they found a key. It opened the garage door.

Moreover, an expert inspection revealed that the garage doors could be opened even without a key.

Although the garage keeper stuck to his story, he admitted that ordinarily, and on the evening of the 22nd, he left the place at 6 p.m. and did not return until 10. Thus there had been ample time for Allaway to open the door and take the car.

Officers located a long letter which the prisoner had written his wife during the war. This disclosed numerous similarities with the handwriting of the telegrams.

Humphries, the motor designer, picked Allaway from a group of other chauffeurs and identified him as the man he saw sitting in the Mercedes.

Waters, listening to each of the chauffeurs repeat the words "Car—car will meet," identified Allaway's voice as the one she heard over the telephone and at the Boscombe post office.

The prisoner was asked to write out the telegrams from dictation. He changed his style of writing during these tests, but failed to correct his spelling. In both the telegrams and these samples written after his arrest, "advertisement" became "advertisment," "pleasant" became "plesant," "expense" became "expence," and "Bournemouth" became "Bournmoth."

G.F. Gurrin, a handwriting expert, scrutinized the specimens of Allaway's writing, including a statement he had written in efforts to clear himself of the charge. Gurrin cut out words and letters from facsimile reproductions, and from these he compiled a chart showing how each looked in the decoy telegrams, in the known handwriting of Allaway before the murder, and in his known handwriting after the murder.

In the word "will," for example, no fewer than 14 comparisons were found. In the word "London," Gurrin noticed at least 10.

"One of the most remarkable pieces of testimony as to handwriting which has ever been brought before a court of justice," remarked Lord Chief Justice Avory after he heard a jury convict the defendant of murder.

The verdict was confirmed on appeal, and his execution was carried out on the morning of Aug. 21, 1922, at the Winchester Prison.

Nothing in this story has been said about motive. What was the motive? No one can say exactly. Apparently it was simply the urge to kill a woman. There have been many cases in which nothing more motivated the murderer. In this instance, Allaway showed the instincts of a serial killer. Had he been more clever and remained insatiated, there is no telling how many London nurses, cooks and other assorted domestics might have disappeared and died.

Vicious Vixen

Joseph McNamara
September 15, 1996

B irdwatchers sloshing through the marshes along the Merrimack River in Newbury, Mass., found the body. The heat of that late spring day, June 2, 1954, and the warm weeks that had preceded it had so badly decomposed the remains that visual identification was impossible.

It remained for fingerprint experts to identify the dead man as Melvin Clark Jr., 29, of Amesbury, Mass. It remained for the medical examiner to determine that Melvin had been stabbed twice in the chest with a narrow, sharp, longish probe and shot in the head twice with a .32-caliber pistol.

Melvin, who was an electronics worker, lived with his wife, Lorraine, and their three young children on the shore of Lake Attitash, where he spent his spare time running a boat-rental service.

Lorraine, 28, had reported Melvin missing on April 11. In fact, she had complained to neighbors in the town of 10,000 souls that Melvin had been cruel to her. And on April 17 she filed suit for divorce.

Finding of the body had, of course, rendered the divorce action null and void. Detectives went to the Clark home, some miles northwest of where the body had been found, to question Lorraine.

She coolly maintained ignorance of how her "abusive" hubby wound up dead in a Newbury marsh.

But when confronted with the body of her missing spouse, Lorraine told a tale of sordid sex, uncontrollable passion, a flaring of anger and murder that had seasoned investigators shaking their heads in wonder. It also had Amesbury in a state of shock.

Lorraine, it was revealed, was a part of a merry band of wife swappers who met periodically at each other's home to try, among other things, a little green on the other side of the fence.

The wives giddily would drop their house keys into a hat of love, and the husbands would take their random pick of keys, which would determine whose little honey they would bed that night.

The swapping of mates was then making a sensational debut as America eased its scruples after the denials of World War II.

But many people in Amesbury thought of such sleazy practitioners of abandoned love as "them," not "us." Lorraine's story told them differently. Sex was alive and well in Amesbury.

As Lorraine explained it in a signed confession, she had married Melvin when she was 18. Life had been a lark—for a while. Children had come; Marlene, then five, Sally, four, and Michael, two. But as the years lengthened to 10 lovely annums, Lorraine got bored.

The fact that hubby spent every waking moment hard at work at his electronics job and boat-rental duties might have had something to do with it.

In any event, by 1954 Loraine had strayed from the marital pasture. She dated men while her husband worked nights. And she dated other men when Melvin worked days. She was a pushover for the wife-swap parties when she discovered them.

Melvin had no clue to his wife's amorous adventures until the night of April 10, 1954, the eve of Palm Sunday, when he returned home and surprised Lorraine with another man.

As soon as the guy got himself together and sheepishly bowed out of the Clark digs, Lorraine flew into a rage. She ranted at her husband and, in a fit of uncontrollable anger, seized two sharp darning needles and plunged them into Melvin's chest, it was related.

She then reportedly seized a .32-caliber pistol and fired two rounds into Melvin's head.

According to the indictment, Lorraine labored for hours that night to get rid of her husband's body. She trussed the corpse with chicken wire, then rolled it to her car and stashed it in the trunk.

Lorraine then drove six miles to the Merrimack River, where she attached two 15-pound weights to the ankles of Melvin's body and, from a bridge, slid it into the water.

As the wife figured it, the telltale corpse would be carried by the river currents out to sea. But it did not happen that way. The grisly package got hung up on reeds in the marshes in Newbury.

The next day Lorraine reported her husband missing. And a week later she filed the divorce action.

Five days after the body was found, police arrested Lorraine in the slaying of her husband. There were reports that the murder grew out of Lorraine's "uncontrollable passion" for another man. She admitted that she had fallen in love with one of the men upon whom she had bestowed her favors.

In pleading guilty to second-degree murder before the court on Nov. 29, 1954, Lorraine declared that she had acted alone. She was sentenced to life in prison.

A day after Lorraine was sentenced, Arthur Jackson, 23, was handed three years in jail for committing adultery with the admitted slayer. Jackson had portrayed himself as Lorraine's paramour, and he was later to confess intimate details of the sordid romance.

Jackson was freed Jan. 19, 1957, after serving 779 days in jail.

Friends of Lorraine said that she had confessed to slaying Melvin by herself to save her children from scandal. However, kiss-and-tell Jackson's juicy tale of sex with Lorraine upset that plan.

On May 15, 1956, Massachusetts attorney general George Fingold reopened the Clark case amid reports that Lorraine had changed her story and now implicated Jackson in the slaying. Nine days later the Essex County grand jury returned a "no bill" against Jackson.

Lorraine began her term at the women's reformatory at Framingham, Mass., without fanfare. She taught illiterate inmates and worked in the prison greenhouse. She made costume jewelry.

But the wife-swap queen was again in the headlines when a state investigation was launched July 30, 1957, into allegations of sexual perversion and the availability of dope and liquor at the Framingham reformatory, along with charges of favoritism for Lorraine.

State Sen. Francis McCann raised the issue on the State Senate floor July 29, and Corrections Commissioner Arthur Lyman ordered a probe.

"What a mockery of our courts," McCann had said. "A woman steals a $3.98 dress and is jailed, and another who is serving time for murder gets a Cook's tour of the state!"

An escaped prisoner had leveled the vice charges, and two former employees of the reformatory had complained that Lorraine was given kid-glove treatment, including Sunday drives with her family outside reformatory grounds.

Lorraine's attorney said she had been given privileges so she could tell her children, that she had pleaded guilty to killing their father and that the place they had been visiting was not a hospital.

The lawyer explained that their schoolmates had been taunt-ing the Clark children about the crime.

Margaret O'Keefe, acting superintendent at Framingham, said Lorraine was allowed to have a car ride with family members every Sunday but never left the reformatory grounds.

"In winter months Lorraine entertains her children in the liv-ing room of a home on the prison grounds," O'Keefe said. "During the summer she takes them to the pavilion or picnic grounds."

But, said O'Keefe, these privileges were available to all prisoners.

In 1963, Lorraine's life sentence was commuted to 22 years by then-Gov. Endicott Peabody and the state's Executive Council. This made her eligible for parole, and that April 14, gaunt and gray but still attractive, Lorraine walked free after nine years and three days behind bars. She spent Easter with her kids.

The Man Upstairs

JOSEPH MCNAMARA
JANUARY 3, 1988

Big Jim Fisk had a magic touch with finances and the blessing of an elastic conscience. In an era of true plunderers he was called The King of Wall Street, a millionaire who flung a flamboy-ant lifestyle across 19th-century New York City. His murder in 1872 over an illicit love and the trial of the accused killer, the "handsom-est man in town," entranced a continent.

It was said, possibly without hyperbole, that at the time of the shooting in Manhattan's Grand Central Hotel, no one in the land was better known save President U.S. Grant. Dubbed Jubilee Jim, this former Vermont peddler, this self-appointed admiral, this huckster supreme died a titan at age 37.

Fisk's New York had a population of 973,106, centered in the area of East Broadway and Grand Street, run by a mayor earning $12,000 a year, aided and abetted by 22 aldermen. Some 5,000 prostitutes in 600 bawdy houses and faro dealers in 200 dens cheered up the gentry.

A big night could be had at Harry Hill's, at Houston and Mulberry streets, the best-run dance house in town, or at The Atlantic Garden, a German beer hall on The Bowery, then alive with the jingle of horse-drawn carts and the crack of rifles in shooting galleries. New York was wild and brash, just made for Jim Fisk.

Perhaps nothing better illustrates the mettle of Big Jim than his caper in Confederate bonds. He was well aware that the Civil War was winding down, for he had closely watched the movement of the army. He had to. He ran cotton from the South, where it sold for 12 cents a pound, to the North, where speculators had driven the price up to $2.

With Boston financiers, Fisk set at Halifax a speedy ship with steam up night and day. When Lee surrendered on April 9, 1865, Fisk telegraphed and the ship set out for London. There, a Fisk operative sold $5 million in Confederate bonds to the English four days before the mail ship arrived with news that there was no longer a Confederacy.

Born April 1, 1834, in Bennington, Vt., James Fisk Jr. ran away from home early on, because his father made him clean stables, and joined the Van Amburg circus—where he cleaned up after elephants. After that, dad's tin-peddler business did not seem so bad. Soon that business had expanded into silks and shawls, jewelry and silverware. Big Jim got four white steeds and a colorful rig. He wore a top hat and cracked a long whip. Every day was circus day.

At 27, he became a salesman for Jordan & Marsh in Boston, and when war flared, he sold J & M blankets to the government and began to understand something useful. "You can sell the government anything," Jim said in wonder.

With the seed money from his Confederate bond coup, he moved to New York and threw in with young Jay Gould, with whose assistance he soon had control of the Erie Railroad. As Prince of the Erie, a title he loved, Fisk bought Pike's Opera House at 23rd Street and Eighth Avenue and renamed it the Grand Opera. Downstairs he ran the opera, upstairs he ran the Erie.

Next, he took over the Narragansett Steamship Line and appointed himself an admiral. He was also a colonel of the Ninth Regiment, National Guard of New York, a station given him when he assumed the unit's debts. He wore his uniforms often.

In 1868 he met Josie.

Josie was Helen Josephine Mansfield, a bustworthy San Franciscan, 27 years old, popularly known as The Mansfield. In her day she was thought of as seductive and beautiful, though surviving likenesses raise questions. In any event, Jubilee Jim looked into those dark gray eyes and was lost. He called her "Dolly." She called him "Sardines."

In short order, Fisk set up Dolly in a mansion near his own on fashionable W. 23rd Street.

"Right royal nest it was for this bird of Paradise," a contemporary wrote of The Mansfield. Fisk's wife, Lucy, meanwhile, lived a separate existence on Boston's Chester Square.

In time, Josie, an actress of sorts with a disastrous marriage behind her, found that Big Jim liked to dally with French actresses from the opera house. She simmered, and when Edward S. Stokes, a business protégé of Fisk's and a man from a fine Philadelphia family, began paying court, she discovered she was ripe for conquest, again.

In August 1870, a distressed Fisk confronted Josie and ordered her to choose. She refused. Broke by October, she contacted Jim and suggested reconciliation. Love, however, had flown.

"You will excuse me if I decline your modest request for a still further disbursement of $25,000," Sardines wrote Dolly.

By year's end, Stokes, who had the instincts of a robber baron but not the talent, needed money, too. He convinced Josie she should cash in on her love letters from Fisk.

Shunning the blatancy of blackmail, the pair launched several suits against Fisk with the letters held over his head. The letters were not sexual blockbusters. They merely made Jim Fisk look like a fool. Stokes picked up a few thousand dollars.

But by late 1871, Fisk was on the counterattack. He got an injunction prohibiting Stokes and Josie from releasing the letters. Further, he obtained an affidavit from Richard King, butler at Josie's love nest. King swore he overheard the dark-haired siren plotting with Stokes to blackmail Fisk for $200,000. The two of them, he said, were living together. Big Jim gave the affidavit to the newspapers in November. Stokes, infuriated, sued for libel.

At the initial hearing in Yorkville Court on Nov. 25, Josie refused to testify against Big Jim Fisk; so powerful was he in 1871 New York City that even Tammany Boss Bill Tweed trembled before him. The hearing was continued to Jan. 6.

What an occasion that was. Stokes was elegantly garbed. Josie's finery was magnificent. But Fisk wore his admiral's uniform. The paper painted Josie as a prostitute, Stokes her "fancy man." Stokes, accustomed to being in the society columns, was livid. His rage increased at luncheon, when he learned that Fisk had been acquitted, that he and Josie had been indicted for attempted blackmail and that arrest warrants were out for them.

In court that morning Stokes had overheard Fisk say he was going to the Grand Central Hotel in the evening to visit the widow of a friend who had recently drowned.

Right on time, Fisk's grand carriage with matched black and white horses swept up to the hotel, at Broadway, Bleecker and Mercer streets. Big Jim started up the staircase. At the top of it stood Stokes, a pearl-handled, four-chambered pistol in his right hand.

"At last I've got you!" Stokes cried as he fired.

A second shot rang out. "For God's sake, will nobody protect me?" Fisk cried as he tumbled down the richly carpeted stairs.

Stokes fired twice more. Then he tossed the pistol, fled, and got as far as the hotel barber shop, where belathered patrons seized and held him.

Fisk was carried to Room 213 and peeled from his fancy duds, diamond shirt studs and cuff buttons. He had been struck by two bullets: one in the abdomen, the other in an arm. The house doctor concluded that the wounds were not mortal.

"Yes, that's the man who shot me!" Big Jim thundered when Stokes was manhandled into the room.

Assured he would be all right, Fisk nevertheless made a will, leaving the bulk of his vast holdings to his estranged wife, who rushed from Boston by train to see him. At 11 p.m., doctors consulted one another and agreed again that the patient was not in danger.

By 7:00 the following morning, however, it was clear that he was bleeding to death. By 11, he was dead.

In colonel's uniform, Fisk lay in state in a redwood-and-gold casket at the Opera House and was given the funeral of a potentate.

Stokes when on trial in June for first-degree murder, with Josie seated next to his attorney. This trial ended in a hung jury and was followed in January 1873 by a second, at which Stokes was convicted and sentenced to death. The conviction was thrown out by the Court of Appeals, which found insufficient evidence of premeditation, and Stokes went on trial a third time the following October. Josie did not attend.

Stokes' defense was that Fisk was also armed with a pistol. He said that while passing the hotel, he saw in a window a woman he thought he knew and he went in. Finding he was wrong, he continued, he was leaving the hotel when he ran into Fisk and found it necessary to defend himself.

Two bellhops, though, testified that they saw Stokes stealthily approach the stairs, lean over the rail and fire the shots at Fisk. This backed the state's charge of malice aforethought. The jury brought in a verdict of third-degree manslaughter, and Stokes was sentenced to four years in prison.

Released in 1876, he experienced varying fortunes, in silver mining and the restaurant business. He died in 1901.

In 1891 Josie married Robert L. Reade, the rich American brother of the Viscountess Falkaland. They divorced eight years later. Dolly was found languishing in poverty in South Dakota in 1909. Thereafter she lived in Paris on gossamer means. She died in 1931.

Boy Meets Girl by Chance
with Tragic Results

RUTH REYNOLDS

AUGUST 25, 1946

"Who shall decide when doctors disagree?" asked learned, sharp-tongued Alexander Pope more than 250 years ago.

Now, if we may take them at their word, doctors are in disagreement to the point of bewilderment in the face of America's appalling crime problem, the aftermath of World War II that twisted the characters of untold thousands of half-grown boys. Girls, too, as we shall see, have not escaped the deforming pressures of war.

Well, in the Case of the Doll-like Corpse, doctors disagreed.

Two District of Columbia Park Department employees first spied the body of the diminutive girl lying under a willow tree on the well-clipped sward at the edge of the sixth green of the golf course that occupies part of East Potomac Park. The time was early morning of Oct. 6, 1944—the war almost three years old, and the warping of its victims well under way.

There had been a series of unsolved murders in Washington, and the news of this one was sufficient to send patrolmen, detectives and Inspector Robert J. Barrett, assistant superintendent of the Washington police force, to the scene. They found that the girl had been strangled with her own turban.

The body was clad in a brown dress covered by a red coat. Later it was discovered that the victim's underclothing was torn. She had been raped, it appeared, then strangled.

One detective picked up a cigarette butt stained with lipstick near the body. Another found a man's belt about 40 feet away. With these bits of evidence in his pocket, Inspector Barrett ordered a half acre of the park roped off and an inch-by-inch search for further evidence.

While Medical Examiner A. MacDonald made his examination of the body—the girl weighed less than 100 pounds—police set about to identify her. A ring on one finger was initialed "D.B." with the inscription "McDonnell High School, June 1944."

It was simple to ascertain from the school directory that McDonnell High School was in Chippewa Falls, Wis., and a telephone call to authorities revealed that its June 1944, graduates included one girl with the initials "D.B."—Dorothy Berrum—whose parents, Mr. and Mrs. Robert Berrum, lived in Chippewa Falls.

When Berrum described his daughter to police by telephone, they knew that the body in the park was all that remained of his child.

This one brief telephone call disclosed to the police all the "past" which lay behind 17-year-old Dorothy Berrum's arrival in Washington three months before her death.

And what the police learned of Dorothy they might have learned of a hundred thousand teenage Dorothies in a thousand towns like Chippewa Falls.

She had always been a "good girl," her father assured the police, had always minded her parents and the teachers at the Roman Catholic McDonnell High School. It was the war that had turned things upside down. Dorothy was glad to stay at home and help her mother until the war work bug hit her. Berrum had opposed her going to Washington. She had pleaded and begged. Wages were high in the capital.

Finally, when Dorothy and two other Chippewa Falls girls satisfied Civil Service requirements and actually had War Department jobs offered them, Berrum, like many another father, relented and consented to her plan to leave her home to work in a big city. With many an injunction from their parents, Dorothy and her friends set off for Washington in July 1944.

For a time the three Wisconsin girls roomed together in a boarding house. Then Dorothy moved to Arlington Farms, a government housing project for women workers.

With her two hometown friends out of sight and their restraining influence out of mind, Dorothy followed the course of many an experience-hungry youngster. She made dates to go skating, dining and dancing with servicemen who grinned at her on Washington streets. Soon wolf calls no longer made her toss her head and quicken her stride. Dorothy became an easy pickup.

Some of the girls at Arlington Farms were disturbed because Dorothy was "too friendly with men she didn't know." Several times she was rebuked by the housemother for staying out after 2 a.m.

Naturally the 17-year-old loved the city and her new life of freedom, and she wrote glowing letters to her family. But her letters omitted mention of conduct that would have horrified her parents.

On the afternoon of Oct. 5, the day of her death, Dorothy, police learned, had made an engagement to meet two girls on a Washington street corner in the early evening. The two girls failed to appear. Apparently—the police theorized—Dorothy, tired of waiting for them, had gone off with someone else.

The medical examiner said Dorothy had been killed between 9 and 10 p.m. of Oct. 5.

The story of the slaying of Dorothy Berrum took up many columns of space in the Washington newspapers and was avidly read by thousands. One such reader was a Washington taxi driver, Harold W. Thomas.

When he finished his paper, Thomas drove to police head-quarters and, apologetic as a man may be when he's not sure whether he is acting wisely, he laid a pocketknife on the desk and said he thought he knew something about the Berrum murder.

At 9:20 the night before, said Thomas, he had been signaled by a girl who answered Miss Berrum's description and a "pretty drunk" young man who wore the uniform of the Marine Corps.

The girl, said Thomas, directed him to drive to a popular eating place just across the Potomac River. As he started his car, the marine leaned forward and, in a whisper, told him to disregard what the girl had said and to let them out at the golf course. The girl overheard her escort and demurred.

Thomas heard the marine explain to the girl that the taxi bill would run too high if they drove the full distance to the restaurant. Apparently she was satisfied with the explanation.

Thomas stopped his car at the golf course. His fares alighted, chaffed with him a bit and asked him for cigarettes, one for each. The brand which Thomas gave them, police ascertained, was the same as that of the stub found at the scene.

Thomas drove off, leaving the couple in the roadway. As his car jolted to a start, he heard something fall from the rear seat. He stopped, looked into the back of the car and saw an expensive pocketknife of the type called a switchblade, in which several push buttons snap the blades into position automatically.

Since he was certain this knife hadn't been on the seat or the floor of the cab before he picked up the girl and the marine, Thomas was confident that it belonged to one of them. But, looking back, he could not see his late passengers. So he kept the knife—until he read of Miss Berrum's murder.

After hearing the taxi driver's story, Inspector Barrett was convinced that Thomas' fares were Miss Berrum and her slayer.

The inspector had already been considering the idea that the murderer was a marine—for he was certain that the belt found 40 feet from the body was marine general issue. Inked on it was the name "E. Tackas." It had one other distinguishing mark—the buckle prong was slightly off center. Barrett learned at once from marine headquarters that "E. Tackas" was Eugene Tackas of Palmerton, Pa., in the South Pacific, far from the scene of the crime. Well, maybe some other marine had worn Tackas' belt.

Well might Barrett have despaired at the task of hunting for one particular marine in Washington in October 1944, when thousands of men in this branch of the service were stationed in and near Washington. But he tackled the job.

He sent detectives to each of the marine barracks to ask three questions: Who had been out on pass the night of Oct. 5? Who had lost a knife? Who had reported that he had lost his belt?

It was the last question which finally brought detectives to Pfc. Earl Jackson McFarland, 24, who had asked his company commander for a new belt on the morning of Oct. 6.

McFarland told a straightforward story and answered all questions with alacrity.

The marine said he had just returned from New Bern, N.C., where he had attended the funeral of his week-old infant and tried to comfort his wife. Then, in his haste to report back on time, he had left his belt behind.

Yes, on the night of Oct. 5 he had been out on a pass. He had been beltless, he said. Accompanied by Corp. James Lawson Westberry and Pvt. Warren Grant Craven, he had strolled about the Washington waterfront, stopping here and there to drink beers.

In a Ninth St. restaurant they had met another marine and had had their pictures taken by a quickie photo machine. It was outside this place, McFarland remembered, he had spoken to a girl.

Then, leaving the girl, he and one of the boys had gone on to other places on Ninth St. for more beer.

"Do you own a switchblade knife?" McFarland was asked.

"No, sir."

"And you didn't wear a belt?"

"No, sir; up to that night, the uniform of the day didn't require a belt."

The detective considered it advisable to test the truth of McFarland's statements through his friends, Corp. Westberry and Pvt. Craven.

"He did have a knife—a push-button knife. I remember him snapping the blades as we walked along," said Pvt. Craven.

That was bad for McFarland, but what Westberry said was worse.

"And after Mac had been drinking a while on Ninth St., he spoke to a girl outside the place," said Westberry. "Mac took her arm. She laughed and offered no resistance. So I said, 'Three's a crowd,' and left."

Corp. Westberry gave McFarland the lie direct.

"Oh, yes, Mac was wearing a belt. Here's the picture we had taken in the quickie joint that proves it," said Westberry.

Barrett almost snatched the cheap little photograph from the corporal's hand! There was a belt about the slim waist of the youth who had just told the police he was beltless when the picture was taken.

In the meantime, another detective had talked with marine Pfc. John S. Holzberger. Holzberger said that some three months before, he had lent McFarland his switchblade knife. Later, Holzberger identified as his own the knife which Thomas had given the police.

With these three pieces of circumstantial evidence in their possession, the police arrested McFarland 36 hours after the murder. He protested his innocence and, but for the evidence they held, the detectives might have found it hard to believe this pleasing fellow was a rapist and murderer.

Lewis Bailey, guard at a Washington building, came forward to say that on the night of Oct. 5 he was parked with a young woman in his car in the park. He saw a drunken marine stagger out of the park. Later, he saw a girl who answered Miss Berrum's description standing behind a parked automobile with a man in civilian clothes. Bailey had not called his companion's attention to the pair and police did not place much reliance in his unsupported word.

But taxi driver Thomas could not identify McFarland, and the authorities had to reckon with the disturbing fact that the name of E. Tackas was on the belt.

Finally, word came from Tackas at his Pacific post that the belt might have been among articles stolen from his duffel bag while he had been a patient in a Melbourne, Australia, hospital.

The police cheered up when they discovered that McFarland was in the same Melbourne hospital at the same time, and they decided, without bothering to seek proof, that McFarland had stolen the bag and had appropriated the belt later found on the links.

It must be said that McFarland's record was all against him. Before he joined the Marines, he was a juvenile delinquent.

Even the name he used was not his own. McFarland's real name was Earl Jack Dills. Born in Maryville, Tenn., 16 miles south of Knoxville, he was the fifth child in a brood of seven. When Earl was seven, his mother died. A few months later, his baby sister and brother died. Earl was handed about by various older members of the family. At the age of 11, he was in trouble.

A grocery store near Mascot, Tenn., where Earl was living, was burglarized. The burglar took candy and gum but left his fingerprints. One print showed a scar. Earl, arrested, had a scar that matched the print.

The frightened little kid was tried before Knoxville County juvenile judge Hu B. Webster. He was sentenced to four years in the State Training School at Nashville.

Earl later said that he "broke out" of that reform school 10 times. But his sister, Mrs. John L. Emory, declared that what Earl called "breaks" were actually releases. In any event, after each break or release, Earl was accused of fresh crimes, including housebreaking and theft.

Earl celebrated his 16th birthday in training school, and it was about that time his father died. Released soon after, the boy swore he was 18, and enlisted in the Army. His age discovered, he was returned to the training school.

During his next break, or release, he stole a motion picture projector from the Mascot school, which he had attended. This time he was sentenced to five years in the state penitentiary.

After serving 31 months, he was released Sept. 8, 1940, on good behavior. Soon after this release, he was accused of robbing a New Market, Tenn., grocery, and was given a workhouse sentence. Mostly, he was guilty of the crimes and misdemeanors of which he was accused. Occasionally, he was not. The police did form a habit of picking on the bad boy.

After his workhouse term, Earl adopted the name "McFarland," which was his mother's maiden name. Under this name he joined the marines. That was in September 1941. He was then 21.

With his new name and in his new uniform, McFarland shook off his old ways. A few months after his enlistment, he met a girl—a nice girl—Doris Mae Dudley of New Bern, N.C. They were married in May 1942. In June he was on his way to Guadalcanal.

McFarland's outfit, the famous First Marine Division, won a presidential citation for valor at Guadalcanal. Men in McFarland's company said he did valiant work as an assault engineer.

We can only conjecture what effect the daily work of war may have had upon this small-town bad boy as he fought from bloody Guadalcanal through the Tulagi and Cape Gloucester campaigns.

Then he contracted malaria and, all in all, he was hospitalized 28 times with malarial seizures.

In September 1943, McFarland was sent to the Melbourne hospital and two months later shipped home as unfit for active duty.

"He and his wife came to us while he was on sick leave," said his sister, Mrs. Emory. "He was more quiet, but he was more nervous than he had been when he left. He wanted to go back overseas. He went to Asheville for a physical examination, but he couldn't pass the test. So he was sent to Parris Island and then to the Washington barracks for guard duty." His wife did not accompany him to Washington because she was expecting a child.

Earl visited his wife about once a month at her parents' home in New Bern, and while he was with her, he was a loving, anxious husband, much on his good behavior, the neighbors said. But back in Washington, the police learned, he behaved quite differently. He got into several minor scrapes and consorted constantly with prostitutes—all of whom, incidentally, had a kind word to say for him.

Late in September, McFarland went to New Bern when his child was born and was highly nervous throughout this ordeal. One week later, he returned for the funeral. That was on Sunday. The following Friday, Dorothy Berrum was killed.

"I didn't kill nobody," McFarland sullenly insisted after his arrest. Swiftly he was indicted on three counts—criminal assault, first-degree murder and murder while committing a felony.

In the meantime, a waitress identified McFarland as the companion of Margaret Fitzwater the night her throat was slashed and her nude body was thrown into a Washington lagoon. That was three weeks before the Berrum murder.

McFarland was indicted again, this time for the rape-slaying of Fitzwater. The indictment was based on a flimsy identification. Police do like to have a double hold on a man whenever possible.

Although the knife which Holzberger had lent McFarland was examined in the laboratories of the Federal Bureau of Investigation, no trace of blood was found on it. Furthermore, police had said originally that Fitzwater's throat was slashed by a knife with a hooked end. Holzberger's knife was straight.

Several months later, McFarland was placed on trial before Justice James M. Proctor in Federal District Court for the murder of Dorothy Berrum.

The prosecutor, U.S. Attorney Edward M. Curran, was ready with a splendid case of circumstantial evidence. The defense counsel, P. Bateman Ennis, and his associate, George A. Cassidy Jr., prepared a case based on the contention that the young man was innocent on the likelihood that, if he were guilty, he was a tragic product of the war.

The prosecution offered many bits of circumstantial evidence, but it was one tiny clue which rose to giant size to damn McFarland.

The celebrated Dr. Wilmer Souder of the Crime Detection Laboratory of the Bureau of Standards positively identified the belt found at the crime scene with the one McFarland was wearing when he and his friends had their photographs taken a few hours before the murder.

And it was the smallest part of the belt, the little prong in the buckle, which made Dr. Souder certain. The prong of the belt was bent one-eighth inch away from center. And the photograph showed the belt prong bent this same distance in the same direction.

To the jury, when he had the opportunity, Ennis insisted that McFarland was innocent. But he urged the jury to consider that if McFarland did commit the crime, he was a sick man and mentally irresponsible as the victim of both malaria and war neuroses.

Then the doctors disagreed.

Dr. Thomas Vernon Moore of Catholic University, priest and psychiatrist, said that his examination indicated that the 24-year-old Guadalcanal veteran was suffering from a mental illness accompanied by a loss of memory. Dr. Moore said that if McFarland suffered from "malarial psychosis," it would be possible for him to recall certain things while others would be forgotten.

Dr. Gregory Zilborg, New York psychiatrist, another defense witness, testified that he considered McFarland mentally ill.

To back this medical testimony, McFarland's commanding officer, Col. Charles Dunbeck, testified that the young marine was, within his own observation, subject to mental attacks brought on by malaria. He called McFarland "one of the floating population of casuals serving on guard duty when fit to do so."

But four of the government's men of medicine assured the jury that McFarland was sane and fully accountable for all his acts. To back their testimony, Assistant U.S. Attorney John W. Fihelly showed the jury the photograph taken the night of the slaying. It showed the marine "smiling and having a dandy time—a fine picture of a man with malaria psychosis!"

Fihelly demanded death in the electric chair. Ennis begged for a verdict of "not guilty by reason of insanity."

An hour and a half after hearing Justice Proctor's charge, the jury brought in a verdict of murder in the perpetration of a felony, which carries a mandatory death sentence.

The judge sent the jurors back to consider another indictment, criminal assault, and they soon returned with a verdict of guilty on that count also.

Then, and not until then, did Ennis learn of Lewis Bailey, the guard in the Capitol who said he saw a marine stagger out of the park some 45 minutes before he saw a girl answering Dorothy's description with a civilian. Promptly, Ennis sought a new trial on new evidence.

"I put no reliance in this alibi testimony," said Justice Proctor. "This type of witness appears in every case of this sort."

Ennis continued to fight, valiantly but vainly, through the courts for a new trial or a sanity hearing for his client.

Then, in April 1943, McFarland sought to help himself—and made his plight worse than ever before, if that were possible. In the company of Joseph D. Medley, another convicted killer, he escaped from the District of Columbia jail. Medley was captured immediately, McFarland eight days later.

Now, appeals for McFarland's life went to President Truman. They included one from Judge Hu Webster, the juvenile court judge who had first sent the boy to a reform school.

With what some called "moral courage" and others called "mushy thinking," Judge Webster said:

"It appears that I failed this man whom I tried in his youth."

Truman, unmoved, denied executive clemency.

The electrocution was finally set for July 19, 1946.

As one newspaper writer, who witnessed the execution, put it: "The young man's courage at the last was unmarred by any suggestion of braggadocio. It appeared rather as the last, desperate effort of a man who was 'shooting the works' to gain, before he died, a fleeting measure of respect from the society which had demanded his life."

Mystery

Mystery is the paprika of crime literature. Although it's satisfying to know the truth, there is something about the unknown that spikes our interest.

Did Lizzie Borden really give mom those 40 fatal whacks of the ax? Who was it in the shadows of the life of beautiful Elizabeth Short who brought the Black Dahlia to prominence?

Was sex behind the slaying of handsome film director Desmond Taylor? It was certainly in front of him daily.

Just who was Jack the Ripper, that rogue of Victorian England who punished ladies of the evening with frightful and painful death.

Some cases will never be solved, of course. And quite probably, that is the secret of their undying popularity.

The Mystery and Myth of Lizzie Borden

JOSEPH MCNAMARA
DECEMBER 27, 1987

I f America has a classic crime, it is probably the Lizzie Borden case. Perhaps the Borden "riddle" would be a better word, for

no crime in our history has been so hotly debated. Several genera-
tions of schoolgirls have skipped rope to the chant:

Lizzie Borden took an ax
And gave her mother forty whacks.
When she saw what she had done
She gave her father forty-one.

Even the facts have been deep-sixed in favor of the legend. For
if indeed Lizzie did take an ax to her stepmother, she stopped at 20
whacks. And dear old dad suffered no more than 10. Then there are
several small technicalities: Lizzie Borden was acquitted by a jury
that deliberated only an hour and 16 minutes, and though it was
suspected, it was never proven that an ax was used.

Although Lizzie died 60 years ago, she has over the years been
convicted and exonerated of the Gay Nineties' vicious double murder in book, novel, play, movie, ballet and even opera. The tug on
America's consciousness seems unlimited.

It all began on the hot Thursday morning of Aug. 4, 1892, in
Fall River, Mass. Andrew J. Borden, 70, an investment banker who
had made his money as a young undertaker, lived a block off Main
Street Residing with him were spinster daughters Lizabeth "Lizzie,"
then 32, and Emma, 37; his second wife, Abigail, 64; a temporary
guest, John V. Morse, 60, brother of Borden's first wife, dearly departed; and the family maid, Bridget "Maggie" Sullivan, 28.

Maggie served Andrew, Abby and John a breakfast of warmed-
over mutton stew, mutton cakes, coffee and bananas—what a last
meal! And Uncle John—as Emma and Lizzie called him—left the
house at 7:45 a.m. to visit other relatives in Fall River. Stern-faced
Borden walked to his office. He once boasted he had never borrowed a dollar, and critics said he had never spent one either.

Emma had gone to visit friends in Fairhaven, 15 miles away. Afterward, by herself, Lizzie had cookies and coffee. In fact, the two daughters ate their meals by themselves since they could not stand their somber 200-pound stepmother, whom Emma called Abby and Lizzie called Mrs. Borden.

Abby told Maggie to wash the windows, and then she went upstairs to the guest room to change John's pillowcases. At 10:50 a.m. Borden unexpectedly returned home, which he rarely did before suppertime.

Borden found the front door locked, which was unusual, and Maggie let him in. She said later she heard Lizzie "laugh on the stairs."

Lizzie told her father that Mrs. Borden had received a note and had gone to visit a sick neighbor. She did not know who the note was from but said she had burned it. While her father went into the living room to lie down, Lizzie ironed handkerchiefs. She told Maggie about a sale of dress goods for eight cents a yard, but the maid said she felt ill and went up the back stairs to her third-floor rear room to lie down.

Maggie heard the City Hall clock strike 11 o'clock. Ten minutes later she heard Lizzie scream:

"Maggie . . . come down quick, father's dead . . . someone came in and killed him!"

Maggie found Lizzie in the hall and was sent to summon Dr. S.W. Bowen from across the street. He was out, so Maggie left word. Lizzie then sent Maggie to get Alice Russell, a neighbor and close friend.

All, including the doctor and a policeman, arrived about the same time and found Borden lying on the living room sofa, his feet on the floor. His head had been beaten so horribly, he was unrecognizable. His wife was found on her knees facedown on the floor of the guest room, her head badly battered, her blood congealing on the floor.

Dr. Bowen believed Abby had been killed an hour before Borden had been attacked from behind with an ax or hatchet.

Both rooms were drenched with blood, the gore spattered on walls and ceilings. The house was searched for weapons and bloody garments. Two axes and two hatchets were found. None was bloodstained, but one ax had no handle and was covered with ashes, which some believed had absorbed the blood. No bloodied garment was found, nor had anyone seen blood on Lizzie, Maggie or Uncle John, who returned unknowingly to the house during the uproar and calmly stopped to munch a pear from the backyard orchard.

There was talk that a druggist could swear that Lizzie had bought poison. The family was ill the day before the slayings, and Lizzie had confided to Alice Russell that she feared the milk had been poisoned.

"I think my father has an enemy," she had told Russell. "He had trouble with a man the other day."

Two weeks later Lizzie was arrested. She protested her innocence, and most of the 75,000 townsfolk supported her. They could not accept that this prim Congregationalist Sunday school teacher, who preached that the way to hell was paved with playing cards and dancing, would wield a fatal ax.

Oddly, many zeroed in on poor Uncle John. When he went to the post office, a crowd of 1,000 surrounded him and shouted, "Murderer!"

Despite Maggie's claim that Lizzie was on the stairs when Borden came in, Lizzie insisted she was in the kitchen. Then she said she went to the barn, behind the orchard, for about 30 minutes to look for a lead sinker to take on a fishing vacation.

On June 5, 1893, Lizzie went on trial in New Bedford. It lasted 13 days. The state charged that Lizzie killed Abby to keep her from inheriting Borden's $500,000 estate, a fabulous sum then, and the father was killed when he came home suddenly.

The case was circumstantial, pegged largely on Lizzie's conflicting statements. But some of her statements were suppressed through the nimble defense of George Robinson, three-time governor of Massachusetts, whom Lizzie paid the princely sum of $500 a day.

It was revealed through testimony that Lizzie had burned a dress in the kitchen stove several days after the slayings. The peppery Lizzie had insisted there was paint on the dress. But a painter who had worked at the house testified that Lizzie's dress had been paint-stained months before.

The state argued that Lizzie had tried to get Maggie out of the house to attend the sale, and they disregarded her alibi about looking for a sinker in the barn. Lizzie never took the stand. She was acquitted on June 20.

Soon afterward, a local reporter wrote "The Fall River Tragedy," laying the guilt squarely on Lizzie. This book influenced other writers—who have mostly convicted rather than acquitted her.

Lizzie vowed never to leave Fall River, and she did not. With her sister, Emma, she lived in seclusion in another house for 14 years. She ignored town gossip, which had turned against her, and stopped going to church. She devoted herself to animal causes.

Then the sisters quarreled, and Emma moved to Providence, R.I. The dispute was never explained, but Emma insisted it had nothing to do with the murders.

Lizzie died June 2, 1927, leaving nothing to Emma. It didn't matter: Emma died 10 days later.

In 1929 the Borden barn was razed, and an old, rusty, stained ax fell into the debris. It rekindled interest in the murders.

Last of the principals, Maggie Sullivan, died in Montana in 1948, taking with her whatever she knew about that now-dim day in 1892 and leaving it all to the writers and the legend.

The "Black Dahlia" Murder

JOSEPH MCNAMARA
MAY 20, 1984

When the nude body of curvy, movie-struck Elizabeth "Beth" Short was found, severed at the waist, in a weed-strewn lot Jan. 15, 1947, it spawned one of the greatest manhunts in the history of Los Angeles. The gruesome slaying of the raven-haired beauty, nicknamed the Black Dahlia, touched a romantic nerve in postwar America, launched a flood of headlines nationwide and called forth a procession of weirdos and publicity nuts.

At last count, more than 40 persons have confessed to the sensational murder—more bogus admissions than in any other case in the annals of California crime. Legions of helpful amateur detectives offered "solutions" to the puzzling case.

"You can have a theory for each day of the year, and if you divide the days in half, you can have twice as many theories," homicide Detective Sgt. Kirk Mellecker, who had headed the case for eight years, told *The News.* "We've heard most of them."

Yet the killer remains at large, unless claimed by death in the intervening years.

It is ironic that the attention and recognition that 22-year-old Beth Short so vainly sought in her quest of a film career came to her only after death. Even the eye-catching moniker "Black Dahlia" seems to have been conferred on her by an enterprising newspaper rewrite man after her slaying, although some acquaintances have come forward to say she was so named because of her fondness for black attire, especially filmy gowns.

To her friends she was mostly Beth, with lovely skin and gray-green eyes that captivated men. She had no name when found in two pieces that Wednesday morning by a horrified pedestrian on South Norton Ave. Her head was bruised, her mouth and breasts were slashed. Her lower body had been mutilated by a knife. And rope burns marked her wrists and ankles. That she had been held prisoner and tortured before death was obvious to detectives.

Why was she dissected, so neatly that vital organs were untouched? One theory was so that she could be transported more easily. Tire tracks nearby indicated she had been taken to the lot by auto. But the Dahlia was only 5-feet-3, 105 pounds. Surely her killer might tote 105 pounds. Unless the slayer was a woman, it was pointed out.

A vengeful lesbian, furious at being repulsed by the Dahlia, was one theory that has been advanced about the slayer. Another was that she had been killed by a sadistic pickup—and pickups were the Dahlia's specialty. Or a possible extortion victim who mutilated the pretty drifter to make it appear to be a sex killing. Maybe a mortician helper or someone with a knowledge of anatomy. All theories. One a day.

Even before she was identified, homicide detectives were be-
sieged with requests to see the body, to speculate on who she was.
Within 24 hours, FBI fingerprint files identified her as Elizabeth
Short, born July 29, 1924, in Hyde Park, Mass., one of four daughters of Cleo and Phoebe Short.

Beth's father had divorced her mother in 1939 and moved to
California, and two years later the girl joined him in Vallejo. However, Short, a navy yard worker, found it difficult to cope with his
high-spirited daughter, who had an inordinate fondness for servicemen. Picked up by juvenile authorities for late hours and sundry
peccadillos, she was shipped back to her mother.

But Beth liked California, and she returned soon. In 1943-44,
she worked as a civilian employee in the post exchange at Camp
Cooke. Her fingerprinting for this job later helped in the identification of her body.

Beth fell in love with an air corps major, Matt Gordon, who
was later killed in action. There was also an army lieutenant. And a
marine was in the picture. Beth, it seems, did more than her part
for the war effort.

But there was also the matter of earning a living. Though ambitious, she was unskilled and had to compete with hundreds of
other stunners seeking fame in Hollywood. She became a familiar
figure to bartenders and waitresses in cafes there.

With discovery of the body, scores of detectives under
homicide's Capt. Jack Donohoe were assigned to the case, and they
quickly pieced together the last days of the Black Dahlia. She had
lived with girl roommates in and around Los Angeles and San
Diego, mostly as their guest. Between such stays, she often slept in
her fetching black clothes in all-night movie houses.

On Jan. 8, the Dahlia left the San Diego home, where she had been living for about a month with yet another roommate, and was driven to L.A. by a man whom the roommate knew only as "Red." He turned out to be a former army musician who helped her deposit her luggage at a bus depot in L.A. the next day and drove out of her life. He had an alibi for the time of the slaying.

A girl acquaintance said that six days before the murder, she saw Beth in an apartment hotel lobby embracing a young man "dressed like a gas station attendant." She was seen in bars five and four days before she died, and one barkeep said her gay vivaciousness had recently turned to sadness. She was spotted at various other places up until 5:30 p.m. of the day before her body was found. When last seen, she was with a busty 6-foot blond woman who appeared vexed when Beth flirted with men, according to homicide detectives.

But the all-important question of where the Black Dahlia had spent the night—and with whom—has defied intensive investigation.

Word of the killing was hardly on the street before suspects were being rounded up. One man was hauled off a bus in Merced, Calif., because as he slept in his seat, he mumbled, "I forgot to cut the scar off her leg." But he had an airtight alibi.

And then the cranks started confessing. But on Friday, Jan. 24, 1947, postal authorities intercepted an envelope addressed to local newspapers. The address and message were made of letters cut from newspapers and pasted on the envelope.

"Here is Dahlia's belongings. Letter to follow," was the cryptic message. Inside were clippings of the death of Beth's air corps major in India, her birth certificate, her ID card and Social Security card, comb and make-up kit and a black address book, all obviously from her purse.

In the book were 76 names, addresses and phone numbers of people Beth knew during her hurried, frantic chase of success. It was a motley group; some in the film world, others not. But investigators failed to link any to the sordid crime.

The letter reeked of gasoline. Probers thought of the sighting of Beth in a clinch with a man "dressed like a gas station attendant" in the hotel lobby, and the pace of the probe quickened.

Four more pasted-letter notes followed. "Dahlia killer cracking. Wants terms," read one. Another: "I will give up in Dahlia killing if I get 10 years. Don't try to find me."

Soon came this: "Here it is. Turning in Wednesday, Jan. 29 at 10 a.m. Had my fun at police—Black Dahlia avenger." The last read: "I'm afraid I won't get a fair deal. Dahlia killing justified."

Officials felt that the letter with the contents of the Dahlia's purse was from either the murderer or someone with intimate knowledge of the crime, and quite possibly, all were from the slayer. With an end to the letters came a distinct setback to hopes of solving the mystery.

There were flares of police interest. A G.I. at Fort Dix, N.J., admitted that he "thought" he had killed the Black Dahlia because he was fearsome when he was drinking. And, he said, he had been in L.A. drinking at the time Beth Short was slain. But not so, it seemed, after investigation. Drinking, yes; in Los Angeles, no.

According to Sgt. Mellecker, the calls have trickled to a near stop. It is a rather cold trail.

'We get a few calls whenever the TV film ["Who Is the Black Dahlia?"] plays on the late show," he said. "We'll investigate any worthwhile lead—the case is still open—but there's not much lately.

As for the wild surge of interest across the country the case generated in its day, the homicide sleuth sees this as indicative of the times, the post–World War II malaise. He adds that there simply was not as much crime then, and we as a people were more easily shocked.

"If it occurred today, the Black Dahlia slaying would be relegated to an inside page," Wallecker declared. "She would not draw nearly as much ink."

Which says something about our reading tastes in the 1980s, perhaps, but even more about the society in which we live.

Was Jack the Ripper the Duke of Clarence?

Kermit Jaediker
January 3, 1971

A surgeon's article stirs a storm of speculation that London's infamous Jack the Ripper was a mad member of Britain's royal family.

On Sept. 27, 1888, the Central News Agency in London's Fleet Street received a letter written by a man who said he disliked prostitutes and spoke, rather gleefully, of killing them:

"Grand work, the last job was. I gave the lady no time to squeal. I saved some of the proper red stuff in a ginger beer bottle over the last job, to write with, but it went thick like glue and I can't use it. Red ink is fit enough. I hope. Ha! Ha! The next job I do I shall clip the lady's ears off and send them to the police, just for jolly."

The letter bore a signature that down to the very present, not only in England but throughout the world, has become a symbol of horror without equal, a nickname for a man, more demon than man, who in 10 frenzied weeks slashed and mutilated five prostitutes to death and then suddenly vanished.

The signature was "Jack the Ripper."

Who was Jack the Ripper?

Over the years, there have been several suspects, all unproven. They include two men who went to the gallows—George Chapman, the wife-poisoner, and Dr. Thomas Neill Cream, who poisoned whores. But the idea that the Ripper ever used poisons is an absurdity. Jack's forte was to jab the lady with a sharp knife and disembowel her.

Sir Melville Macnaghten, who had charge of Scotland Yard's Criminal Investigation Department from 1903 to 1913, expressed the belief that the slayer, himself sickened by the special horror of his last crime, committed suicide. In this connection, Sir Melville strongly suspected Montague Druitt, a young lawyer whose body was fished from the Thames. But Sir Melville conceded that here was a "less likely alternative"—that the killer was found out by his relatives and lodged in a private insane asylum.

A new answer to the 82-year-old riddle, an answer in line with the "less likely alternative," has just been advanced, triggering a controversy that is sweeping England, from the cockney on the street, who is thoroughly enjoying it, to Buckingham Palace, which doesn't enjoy it a bit.

The latest theory is that one of the world's most terrible killers was a nobleman whose brain was addled by syphilis and who once got caught in a raid on a homosexual brothel. The Palace's aversion to this concept of Jack the Ripper is quite understandable, for one theory led to another, that the blue-blooded syphilitic was in direct line of succession to the British throne.

The nobility thesis was put forth by Dr. Thomas Stowell— 88-year-old author and a fellow of the Royal College of Surgeons, in an article in November's issue of *The Criminologist*—a British professional journal of police science. Dr. Stowell said he kept his "evidence" secret for nearly 50 years because he didn't want to involve as witnesses some close friends still alive. Even in his article, Stowell was pretty secretive. He referred to his suspect only as "S."

But he gave enough details about S's family, his life and his "paranoid extravagance of dress" to indicate to any student of British contemporary history (including the *London Sunday Times*, which broke the story) that S was no less a personage than Prince Albert Victor Christian Edward, Duke of Clarence.

The duke was Queen Victoria's grandson. He was the son of Edward VII and Queen Alexandra and elder brother of George V. He was also a great-uncle of Elizabeth II, the reigning queen.

To understand how Stowell came to his sensational conclusion, one must, as Dr. Stowell did in his article, return to the scene of the crimes. Criminologists have attributed to the Ripper as many as 14 murders, including crimes committed after 1888. But Dr. Stowell apparently goes along with Sir Melville's version that "the Whitechapel murderer committed five murders and no more."

According to Tom A. Cullen, whose well-researched book, *When London Walked in Terror,* was published in 1965, the Ripper's hunting ground in the Whitechapel area was a notorious quarter-mile square known as Spitalfields.

One of its landmarks was a churchyard called Itchy Park, on whose benches filthy and diseased derelicts slept off cheap gin drunks. Frequently on those benches would huddle a dozen or so women who, according to one sightseeing guide, "would sell themselves for two pence or a stale loaf of bread." It was on such women, at the very bottom of whoredom, that Jack the Ripper preyed.

His first victim, Mary Ann "Polly" Nicholls, was found dead at 4:14 a.m., Aug. 31, 1888, in a gutter. She was on her back, legs straight out, as though an undertaker had laid her out. The officer who found her felt her arm, which was "warm as a toasted crumpet," indicating death had occurred only a short time before. Her throat had been slashed and she had been disemboweled. There had been no moon. No witnesses were found who could say they had seen her with a man.

Annie "Dark Annie" Chapman, 47, was found, her head almost severed, in the backyard of 29 Hanbury St. at 5:50 a.m., Sept. 8; and this time, although there was no moon, a man thought to be her killer was seen. Twenty minutes earlier, Elizabeth Long, wife of a park keeper, had passed the house and seen a man and woman talking in front of it. Long recognized Dark Annie.

"She thought the man was dark, appeared to be over 40 and was a little taller than Dark Annie," Stowell wrote. "He wore a deerstalker hat.

"After the murder of Annie Chapman, the murderer apparently made his way to Liverpool—how long after it is not known, but I think he may have gone there to escape from the control of his family."

The following note, postmarked 1 Liverpool, Sept. 29, was sent to the police by the Ripper: "Beware, I shall be at work on the first and second in Minorities at midnight and I give the authorities a good chance, but there is never a policeman near when I am at work." The Minorities, a street running north from the Tower of London, was close to Mitre Square.

But apparently wily Jack struck before the Liverpool note could be delivered. On Sunday, Sept. 30, he sent a postcard to the Central News Agency to which he added a bold touch—a bloody thumbprint.

"You'll hear about Saucy Jack's work tomorrow," he wrote. "Double event this time. Number One squealed a bit. Had no time to get ears for police."

Number One, Elizabeth "Long Liz" Stride, 45, was found in Berner St. at about 1 a.m. on Sept. 30 by the owner of a pony-drawn wagon. Her windpipe had been severed, but the slayer, evidently scared off by the approaching wagon, had no time to perform one of his anatomical monstrosities on Long Liz.

Forty-five minutes later, a police constable found a woman's body in Mitre Square. She was Catherine Eddowes, and the slayer's blood-lust must have risen high when he pounced on her. He slashed her throat, tore out her left kidney and uterus, nicked the lower eyelids and cut one ear lobe but got no farther. He may again have been interrupted by some sound.

At 11:45 p.m., said Dr. Stowell, a man named William Marshall saw Long Liz talking to a man described "as mild speaking and well-educated, about 5 feet 6 inches tall, wearing a cutaway coat and gloves."

Then, only 16 minutes before she was found dead, a constable "saw Elizabeth Stride talking to a man of medium height about 28 years of age, clean-shaven and of respectable appearance. He wore a dark overcoat, a dark deerstalker hat and carried a newspaper parcel."

Ten minutes before the discovery of the second corpse, commercial traveler Joseph Lawende saw the Eddowes woman talking to a man at the entrance to Mitre Square. The man was "about 30 years of age, 5 feet 9, with a small fair mustache and wearing a deerstalker hat with a peak in front and behind." This time the man's face was illuminated by a "sickie moon."

"After the murder of Catherine Eddowes," said Stowell, "there was a gap of 39 days instead of the usual 14 before the next murder, during which time I believe the murderer was incarcerated. He evidently escaped, I believe, from a mental home in the Home counties from whence he could get to a main line terminus in London and thus to Whitechapel."

On Nov. 9, the Ripper killed indoors for the first time. He invaded a hovel in Miller's Court and slashed the throat of Mary Jeanette Kelly, like the others a gin-soaked streetwalker, but only 25 and pretty. There were neither gas nor candles, so he made a small bonfire from old clothes, and by its light, went into a knife orgy that made one police official observe that something out of hell must have been loose there.

He cut off the woman's ears and nose and removed her internal organs and scattered them about the room.

Dr. Stowell said that the Ripper was again "put under primate restraint, given such intensive medical care and skilled nursing that he had temporary remissions of his illness . . ." The doctor implied Scotland Yard was aware of all this and deliberately kept it under wraps.

Right after the fifth murder, "Police relaxed their vigilance," senior inspectors assigned to the murder district were withdrawn and special patrols disbanded. Dr. Stowell added that the coroner at the Kelly inquest "chose deliberately to suppress evidence and said so," and Stowell asked: "What were he and the police trying to hide?"

It seemed obvious, Stowell went on, that the police were trying first to prevent more murders and second "to avoid the embarrassment that would be caused by bringing to trial for these murders the heir of a noble and prominent family." Stowell added:

"His activities were probably known to his family after the second murder, perhaps even after the first . . .

"Now for my suspect. I prefer not to name him but to call him S. He was the heir to power and wealth. . . . His grandmother, who outlived him, was very much the stern Victorian matriarch. . . . His father, to whose title he was the heir, was a gay cosmopolitan and did much to improve the status of England internationally. His mother was an unusually beautiful woman with a gracious personal charm. . . .

"After the education traditional for an English aristocrat, at the age of a little over 16 years, S went on a cruise round the world with a number of high-spirited boys. . . . It is recorded that he went to many gay parties ashore. . . . I believe that at one of the many shore parties which he enjoyed in the West Indies on his world journey he became infected with syphilis.

"Some weeks later he had an important public appointment in what was then one of our colonies. At the last moment he canceled that appointment on account of 'a trifling ailment.'

"He arrived back in England before his 19th birthday. At the age of 21 he was given a commission in the Army where he was successful, popular and happy.

"He resigned his commission at about the age of 24. This was shortly after the raiding of some premises in Cleveland Street . . . which were frequented by various aristocrats and well-to-do homosexuals."

Amateur sleuths seeking to tie in S with the Duke of Clarence will find interesting *Edward and the Edwardians,* a book written by Phillippe Jullian.

"Before he died," wrote Jullian, "poor Clarence was a great anxiety to his family. He was quite characterless and would soon have fallen prey to some intrigue or group of rogues, of which his regiment was full.

"They indulged in every form of debauchery and on one occasion the police discovered the duke in a maison de recontre of a particularly equivocal nature during a raid."

The book, first published in 1962, touched, but only touched, upon an area explored by Stowell. "The young man's evil reputation soon spread," wrote Jullian. "The rumor gained ground that he was Jack the Ripper . . . "

Stowell, perhaps inadvertently, dropped another clue. "I have seen a photograph of my suspect which suggests paranoia by the extravagance of his dress, for which I am told he became a butt. In this photograph he is seen by a riverside holding a fishing rod, wearing a tweed knickerbocker suit of perfect cut, not a fold misplaced and without a crease.

"On his head is a tweed cap set far too precisely and he has a small mustache. He is wearing a four to four and a half inch stiff starched collar and is showing two inches of shirt-cuff at each wrist."

There is a photograph of the Duke of Clarence that matches Dr. Stowell's description rather well, except that he's wearing a kilt.

Stowell added that he was told by his elders that S was nicknamed Collar and Cuffs. Clarence had a very long neck, and his father would jokingly tell children in the royal family: "Don't call him Uncle Eddy. Call him Uncle Eddy-Collars-and-Cuffs."

Stowell had studied in youth under Sir William Gull, physician to Queen Victoria, and "to a large number of the aristocracy and the wealthy including, if I am right in my deductions, the family of Jack the Ripper.

"It was said that on more than one occasion Sir William Gull was seen in the neighborhood of Whitechapel on the night of a murder. It would not surprise me to know that he was there for the purpose of certifying the murderer to be insane so that he might be put under restraint as were other lunatics apprehended in connection with murders . . .

"Jack the Ripper was obviously Sir William Gull's patient."

Stowell knew Gull's daughter, Caroline Acland. "Mrs. Acland told me that she had seen in her father's diary an entry, 'informed Blank that his son was dying of syphilis of the brain.'" The date of the entry, said Stowell, was November 1889, after S had returned from a "recuperative voyage."

Clarence died in 1892 at the age of 28 from "influenza complicated by pneumonia." Dr. Stowell did not give the year of S's death but said the cause was broncho-pneumonia—"the usual cause of death in such cases."

Summing up what he called his "evidence," Dr. Stowell said that S was "under medium height and had a fair mustache and wore a deerstalker hat."

S, Stowell pointed out, frequently stalked deer on the family estate in Scotland, and this gave him the chance to watch and, if he wished, to aid in dressing carcasses. Said Stowell:

"The sex instinct of the psychopath is sometimes stimulated by watching dissections or mutilations. This happened to the Ripper. Then later his mind was broken down still further by the poison of the syphilitic infection, and it became directed toward his crimes.

"It is significant to remember that Jack the Ripper wore the deerstalker's hat, as a kind of ritual vestment, when he murdered and mutilated the Spitalfields prostitutes."

When the scandal broke implying that the Duke of Clarence was Jack the Ripper, unnamed sources at Buckingham Palace, residence of Queen Elizabeth, branded the story as "too absurd and ridiculous for comment." Dr. Stowell himself, interviewed on television about Clarence's possible involvement, did not dispute the theory, nor did he confirm it.

Later, still unnamed palace officials, apparently feeling that "absurd and ridiculous" weren't much of an argument, cited old court circular and news clippings to make the claim that on the dates of two of Jack the Ripper's crimes, the Duke of Clarence was shooting in Scotland and celebrating his father's birthday at Sandringham, a royal country residence.

Under pressure of the very row he had cooked up, Dr. Stowell wrote a letter to a London newspaper in which he declared: "I have at no time associated his Royal Highness, the late Duke of Clarence, with the Whitechapel murders or suggested that the murderer was of royal blood. It remains my opinion that he was a scion of a noble family."

Was Dr. Stowell backing down? Or was he merely being very literal when he claimed he had at no time associated Clarence with Jack the Ripper? This was quite true. He hadn't. All he had done was speak of a noble called S. Others brought Clarence into it.

Dr. Stowell's treatise in the *Criminologist* was highly speculative, although there were some rather significant data, such as the Yard's sudden relaxation of its manhunt, right on the heels of the Ripper's most abominable crime. And the doctor's connection with Dr. Gull, physician to the royal family, was fraught with interesting possibilities.

Had Dr. Stowell known more than he had written? If so, the knowledge went with him to the grave. He died a day after sending his letter disclaiming he had ever associated the Ripper with Clarence.

He had left behind a folder entitled "Jack the Ripper," but his son, Dr. I. Eldon Stowell, revealed the file had been burned. He said he had read just enough of the file "to make sure there was nothing of importance." Said the son:

"The family decided that this was the right thing to do. I am not prepared to discuss our grounds for doing so.

"My father left no instructions or request on what we were to do with it. I know that he had been interested in this subject for many years, and that it rose again recently—for what reason I don't know."

No matter how trivial his family considered Dr. Stowell's file, the world would certainly have liked to have had a peek into it. Surely, Scotland Yard would have been interested. And then again, maybe not.

The Mystery of the Cigar Girl

Joseph McNamara
October 5, 1986

Mary C. Rogers became known as the Beautiful Cigar Girl after an enterprising tobacconist hired her to boost sales in his lower-Manhattan shop in early 1840. She lured the eager youngbloods with her dark-haired loveliness and drew repeated purchases from such literary lights as Edgar Allan Poe, Washington Irving, James Fenimore Cooper and Fitz-Greene Halleck.

Halleck was so smitten, he wrote a poem about the tall, willowy Mary. And after she was raped and brutally murdered in 1841,

Poe immortalized her in his short story, "The Mystery of Marie Roget."

New Yorkers were shocked by the crime. Mary had exceeded the fondest hopes of John Anderson when he installed her as clerk in his cigar store on Broadway near Thomas Street. Mary was 20, and her physical charms and winsome ways brought her a legion of admirers.

Mary was five when her father died and left her mother to scratch out a living running a lodging house on Nassau St. Mary helped out, but she found Anderson's offer too generous to resist.

In January 1841, Mary created a sensation by vanishing for a week. The press gave the story great play. When Mary returned, she said she had visited relatives in the country.

Despite her story, it was rumored she had been seen about town with a tall, dark naval officer. Mary, known for her virtue as well as her beauty, became so upset by the rumors that she quit the cigar store and returned to mother.

A month later she was engaged to boarder Daniel Payne, a clerk.

At 10 a.m. on Sunday, July 25, 1841, Mary told her betrothed she was going to spend the day with her aunt, Mrs. Downing, on Bleecker St.

"All right, I'll call for you tonight," Payne said.

But the day was a scorcher—93 in the shade—and Payne sought respite in several neighborhood bars. That evening, a furious thunderstorm dampened any resolve Mary's swain might have had to meet her at Mrs. Downing's. He wobbled home.

Because of the storm, Mary's mother was not perturbed when Mary, now 21, failed to come home. But when she had not returned by the following evening, she sent Payne to check with Mrs. Downing. He was jolted to learn Mary had never arrived there.

Since there was no police missing persons bureau then, Payne inserted a notice in *The Sun* that Mary Rogers was missing. Tuesday passed without word. On Wednesday three men sailing a ketch in the Hudson River off Castle Point, Hoboken, found a woman's body near shore.

A piece of lace had been ripped from the woman's underskirt and was knotted around her throat. Her face had been beaten severely.

Cords bit into both wrists where her fawn kid gloves ended. A portion of her skirt had been used to tie a rock to her waist. Her bonnet hung by ribbons. Her clothing was torn. It was the body of Mary Rogers.

Dr. Richard Cook of Hoboken ruled strangulation the cause of death. He said Mary had been raped.

Castle Point was then a river resort. Nearby was an oasis called Cybil's Cave. There were lemonade stands, beer gardens and a strolling woods for lovers that was named Elysian Fields.

The investigation was put on hold while New Jersey and New York discussed jurisdiction. The latter won. A citizens' group put up $500 to finance the probe.

On Aug. 2, a story appeared in *The Tribune* stating that Mary had been seen on Theater Alley near Broadway with a tall, dark, nattily tailored man, and they walked to Barclay Street, as if to take the Hoboken ferry.

In Hoboken, a Mrs. Loss reported that a couple fitting that description had stopped at her lemonade stand and then gone off toward the Elysian Fields. She said she later heard a scream from the woods, but since strange types often strolled there, she thought nothing of it.

Then a new clue emerged. Joseph Morse, an engraver, had been seen July 25 boarding the Staten Island ferry with a young lady. The next day Morse seemed nervous. He had beaten his wife and vanished.

Nailed Aug. 9 in West Boylston, Mass., he admitted taking a pretty stranger to Staten Island that Sunday morning with lechery on his mind. He even adjusted his watch so that they missed the last ferry back. But when Morse put the moves on, he was soundly clobbered.

He later fled to Massachusetts because he thought his pickup date had been Mary Rogers. However, when his plight became public, his unnamed, unassailable companion of that Sunday afternoon came forward and cleared him.

At this time, Mary's body was exhumed, but the only one fact learned was that the strip of skirt at Mary's waist had been tied with a sailor's knot.

A seaman stationed on the berthed U.S.S. *North Carolina* came under suspicion but was released.

On Sept. 10, Gov. William Seward offered a $500 reward for the killer. The next day, the coroner got an anonymous letter, telling of a rowboat with six "toughs" and a well-dressed woman arriving in Hoboken from New York the morning of the slaying. The girl skipped merrily into the woods and the six followed, the letter added.

Shortly afterward, a boat with three gentlemen landed in the same spot, and one asked two strolling gents if they had seen a woman with six men. Told yes, the boater asked if she had gone willingly into the woods. Again told yes, he got into the boat and returned to Manhattan.

After the letter was published, the two strollers came forward and confirmed its contents. They said they knew Mary Rogers by sight and the woman looked like her, but they were not close enough to be sure.

On Sept. 25 the spot where Mary presumably met her fate was discovered by Mrs. Loss' two young sons while gathering sassafras bark. In a thicket they found a white petticoat, silk scarf, parasol and a linen hankie embroidered "M.R." The items were identified as Mary's. Trampled ground and shrubbery indicated a struggle. A scuffed track, hinting at a dragged body, led toward the river.

Two weeks later, Mary's fiance, Payne, cracked under the strain. His body was found at the assumed spot of Mary's ravishment and murder, an empty laudanum (a narcotic) bottle nearby.

Poe's celebrated story, published in November 1842, moved the slaying to Paris but followed details closely. He suggested the slayer was a handsome young naval officer with whom Mary had been flirting.

In 1851, a pamphlet appeared in New Orleans with the purple title: "A Confession of the Awful and Bloody Transactions in the Life of Charles Wallace, the Fiend-like Murderer of Miss Mary Rogers, the Beautiful Cigar Girl of Broadway, New York."

A foreword by a minister stated Wallace gave him the tale just before a mob burned him and an accomplice at the stake near Memphis, Tenn., for another slaying.

It related that Wallace saved Mary's life in New York when she slipped in the path of an oncoming train at a Harlem railroad depot. Naturally, they fell in love. On July 25, the pair excursioned to Hoboken, repaired to the idyllic wood and Wallace playfully looped a satin cord around Mary's neck. He became a little rough, and she protested: "Others don't treat me that harsh!"

In a fit of rage, Wallace confessed, he tightened the cord until Mary was dead.

Authorities are not sure which was the bigger fiction, Poe's or Wallace's. Truth is, any hope of solving the murder of the Beautiful Cigar Girl is as long gone as Hoboken's Elysian Fields.

A Place to Die Together

RUTH REYNOLDS

SEPTEMBER 27, 1964

Heavy rain between 7 and 8 o'clock on election night may have kept some New Jerseyans from polling booths, but it didn't stay the passionate embrace of a young couple in a coupe parked on bleak Duck Island . . . or deter a murderer with a shotgun.

At 8:30 that evening of Nov. 8, 1938, another couple heard a girl screaming as they drove on Duck Island Road, which wound along the barren strip of filled-in land which separates the Delaware River from the Delaware-Raritan Canal half a mile away. The driver turned his car toward the sound—500 feet up a lovers' lane. His headlights picked up the coupe and a man lying beside it in a puddle of blood and rainwater. The girl, disheveled and critically wounded, was on the seat.

A telephone call brought police from Trenton, six miles north, and patrol cars and an ambulance from Hamilton Township, which includes Duck Island. Wrapped in a blanket, the girl was rushed to St. Francis Hospital. Shot in the abdomen, she was in no condition to be questioned. But she clung to life and police waited at her bedside.

The youth, shot in the chest, was dead. He was identified as Vincenzo "Jimmy" Tonzillo, 20, of Trenton. His wife, Victoria, was an expectant mother. Only a few hours earlier, he had dropped her at a relative's house, kissed her goodbye and set off (she thought) for his night job with a sand and gravel company in Morrisville, Pa., across the Delaware River.

However, Jimmy's brothers were not surprised—for they knew all about his passion for Mary Myatovich, 15. Mary's father, Michael, had warned him to stay away from the kid.

Regaining consciousness briefly, Mary managed to tell her father and detectives that she and Jimmy were seated in his car when a black man appeared and demanded money. Refusing, Tonzillo got out of the car. Mary heard a shot. She saw Jimmy fall. She leaped from the car and tried to escape in the underbrush. The murderer caught her, raped her and shot her.

At 7:15 a.m., Nov. 10, Mary died. Mercer County prosecutor Andrew J. Duch doubted her halting account of what happened. He thought that by blaming "a black," Mary was protecting someone she knew. But the police could find no avengers among the youth's in-laws or the girl's relatives.

They found two 12-gauge shotgun shells at the scene, and they questioned all Hamilton Township shotgun owners, including Clarence Hill, a laborer in a Trenton rubber factory. None admitted owning a 12-gauger.

They also questioned a squatter colony of jobless blacks holed up in an abandoned Delaware River brick kiln. But none of these men owned a gun at all. An investigation of members of a curious cult known as the Scouters was also fruitless. The Scouters were Peeping Toms who got their kicks out of watching the wooing of Duck Island petters.

The Tonzillo-Myatovich slayings discouraged both petters and peepers for a while. Then on a Sunday morning in October 1939, a Trenton "beachcomber" scouring Duck Island for junk kicked at a woman's shoe in a pile of rubbish close to the spot where Tonzillo's body was found 11 months before. There was a woman's body buried in the trash.

She had been shot in the head with a 12-gauge shotgun, a part of her right arm had been blown off and her head had been crushed by a concrete slab. In a car 100 feet away was the body of a young man.

Investigators learned that the dead woman was Katherine "Kitty" Werner, 36. The man was identified as Frank J. Kasper, 28, her husband's best friend. Kasper, a Trenton auto mechanic, had been shot in the head and neck with a 12-gauge shotgun.

For a time, police detained Stanley Werner, 33, father of Kitty's two children. Also, they checked the alibi of Frank's wife, Clara, mother of his five-year-old son.

Clara couldn't believe her husband took Kitty to Duck Island; she thought they must have met accidentally while shopping and were lured there by the murderer. But there was evidence to the contrary.

So, again, the police came up with nothing, except an uncorroborated report that a mystery man, garbed as a minister, had been seen in the area. Hamilton Township police chief R. F. Brettell asked all Duck Island spooners to come forward with reports of any incidents which aroused their suspicions. Nobody responded.

Then Brettell asked the help of the New Jersey State Police, and Detective Sgt. William Horn was assigned to the investigation of the Duck Island murders. It is doubtful if Horn heard immediately what happened to Mr. and Mrs. Joseph Tranatti on the night of Aug. 8, 1940, across the river in Bucks County, Pa.

This young Bristol, Pa., couple, keeping their marriage a secret from their families, were making love in a car parked on Tyburn Road, just outside Morrisville and across from Duck Island, when a black man approached and demanded money. Tranatti managed to get his car in motion at once. No shots were fired.

Three months later, in the same place, a black man approached another parked car and demanded money from Howard Wilson, 19, and Irene Robbins, 18. The youth refused and tried to start his car. The robber raised a shotgun and fired.

Although the shot mangled Wilson's left arm, he managed to get his car going and drove seven miles to Harriman Hospital in Bristol, where he collapsed at the entrance. That was on Nov. 2, 1940.

Fourteen days later, the bodies of Caroline Moriconi, 27, and Louis Kovacs, 36, both of Trenton, were found in a car parked off Cypress Lane in Hamilton Township, three miles south and inland from Duck Island. The pair were in an intimate embrace when Kovacs was shot through the heart with a 12-gauge shotgun and his sweetheart was shot through her heart, lung and left arm.

Another illicit affair! Moriconi's husband, Dante, stood firm through questioning and his alibi was sound. He did not know his wife was playing around with Kovacs, a bachelor.

Now came a pause in murder. For 15 months there were no attacks. And no solutions, either.

On the night of March 7, 1942, Pvt. John Testa, 25, a soldier from Fort Dix, sat with his girl in a car on the Bordentown Ferry Road near Morrisville. A black man fired on Testa and shattered his left arm.

The frightened girl, Antoinette Marcantonio, 21, scrambled from the car. The gunman pursued her, caught her and beat her with the shotgun stock till a piece of it broke off.

Testa was able to start his car in spite of his wound and the gunman ducked into the underbrush to avoid being run down.

Testa and the girl reported the attack immediately. Then the soldier went to the hospital, where his injured arm was amputated.

Next morning, investigators combing the scene, found a shotgun forearm. That part of the gun, which is between the stock and the barrel, bears the serial number of the weapon.

The next mystery is why it took so long to trace that particular shotgun serial number. For more than 18 months passed before Sgt. Horn unearthed from the files of the detective bureau in Trenton a pawn ticket for a shotgun bearing that identical serial number.

Checking the records of a Trenton pawnshop, Horn learned the gun had been pawned seven years before by Martin Keane of Trenton. When Keane was found, he said he had carried the ticket around for almost three years because he had no money to redeem his property.

While working on a WPA project, he opened his wallet one day and the ticket fell out. A black worker known to him only as Clarence, asked for it. Since Keane still didn't have the money to reclaim the gun, he gave Clarence the ticket.

When Horn learned that in 1940 Clarence lived in Hamilton Township at a place about three miles from Duck Island, he called on the township's police captain, Thomas D. Simpson. The only Clarence recalled by Simpson was Clarence Hill, whose father, Wilson, lived in the Broad Street Park area.

Further checking showed Hill to be a laborer of 33. The one mark against him was the desertion of his wife and two children back in 1938. In March 1943, he had been inducted into the army. After training at Indiantown Gap, Pa., he was transferred to Fort Moultrieville in South Carolina. Horn learned Hill was about to be shipped overseas with a heavy truck outfit.

An appeal by Mercer County prosecutor Walter D. Cougle caused Hill to be detained when his unit sailed.

Martin Keane agreed to go to the South Carolina camp with Simpson, Horn and Detective Elmer M. Updike. According to the policemen, their party was passing a group of soldiers at Moultrieville when one shouted, "Hi ya, Red!"

It was Hill hailing Keane, a redhead.

The soldier, a slender man of medium height, was summoned before Col. Elmer S. Van Benscholten, commander at Fort Moultrieville. When the questioning began, he denied knowing Keane and denied any knowledge of the Duck Island killings. He admitted getting the pawn ticket for a shotgun "from somebody."

For a while, he insisted he gave away the ticket. Then he admitted redeeming the gun himself, but said he gave it to a friend . . . he couldn't remember who. Then, according to the colonel, Clarence Hill confessed.

He was transferred to Fort Dix in New Jersey. The questioning began all over again, this time in the presence of Lt. Col. Lewis R. Sussman, provost marshal at Dix.

Again, Hill confessed to the Duck Island slayings.

In giving his account of the Tonzillo-Myatovich killings, he said he bought whiskey and wine and then, for no particular reason, drove to Duck Island in his father's car. He saw the parked car and killed the lovers "because I thought if I killed them, they wouldn't be able to cause me any trouble." He admitted he "used the girl sexually."

Lights of an oncoming car forced him away. He found blood on his trousers, so he burned them with the aid of kerosene in the home of a relative.

He said he hid his shotgun in the woods along Kuser Road near White Horse. It was never found.

Eventually, he was transferred from Fort Dix to police headquarters in Hamilton Township. Over and over, he was questioned
by investigators seeking more explicit details of each murder.

But Hill was vague and gave no definite motive for his crimes.
He had been a fairly steady worker and was never desperate for
money. He drank, but he wasn't a drunkard. He had a capacity for
sex, but he wasn't a maniac.

Finally, he repudiated his story. He had never killed anybody,
he said.

Arraigned in Hamilton Township Police Court on Feb. 8, 1944,
Hill stood impassive in his Army uniform, but without tie, belt or
shoelaces. Recorder Willard F. Grimm read charges signed by
Simpson that Hill "did willfully and feloniously kill." Hill pleaded
not guilty and was remanded to Mercer County Jail in Trenton to
await grand jury action.

His denial of guilt was believed by his lawyers, Frank H.
Wimberley and Robert Queen, the only black attorneys in Trenton,
and they gave him the best they had. When he was indicted on six
counts of murder, they pleaded successfully that the indictments be
dismissed because there were no blacks on the Mercer County grand
jury.

Cougle promptly summoned a grand jury panel that included
blacks, and Hill was indicted anew. Meanwhile, a Bucks County
grand jury at Doylestown, Pa., indicted him for the Wilson-Robbins
and Testa-Marcantonio attacks.

After a long wait, Hill went to trial on Dec. 6, 1944, before an
all-white jury in Mercer County Court for the murder of Mary
Myatovich.

For all the diligent work of Sgt. Horn, the state's case was tenuous.

There was Mary's dying statement that she had been raped and shot by a black man. There were the 12-gauge shells found at the scene. There was Keane's testimony that before this murder, he gave Hill a pawn ticket for a 12-gauge shotgun. There was testimony that a black man beating Miss Marcantoni dropped a piece of a shotgun. There was the forearm of this shotgun on a Pennsylvania road.

Was Hill the Duck Island gunman? The defense said he wasn't—but the defendant's confession said he was.

The high point of the trial came when Hill, on the stand, accused Hamilton Township police of brutality. Cougle objected to this testimony on the ground that it was irrelevant, since the defendant had previously confessed at Moultrieville and Dix.

The jury was excused, and Hill told his story to the judge. Judge Frank S. Katzenbach III decided the defendant's testimony was relevant. The jurors were recalled and Hill told them a false confession was beaten out of him while he was questioned in Hamilton Township police headquarters. Said Hill:

"State Police Sgt. William Horn ordered me to remove my clothes and Capt. Thomas Simpson laid three clubs on the table. Sgt. Horn told me to keep my hands up and he struck me on the left side of my head with a club.

"I dropped my arms a bit, and Capt. Simpson pumped right and left with his fists into my ribs. When I couldn't hold up my hands any longer, Sgt. Horn beat them back.

"He beat them back!" the trembling defendant shrieked. "I'll never forget it to the day I die!"

Hill's voice faltered. His mother cried aloud. Spectators wept.

Did the police beat him to get more details out of him?

One by one, the New Jersey policemen said they never laid a hand on Hill. The two army men present at the questionings said the prisoner was treated well in spite of his confessions of monstrous guilt.

In his defense, various members of Hill's respectable family testified he was with them at their Trenton voting place between 7 and 8 p.m. on Nov. 8, 1938.

The Rev. William H. Turner of the Mount Olivet Baptist Church said that for two years the defendant was a Sunday school superintendent and that his reputation was good.

A jury of seven men and five women deliberated from 4:38 p.m. to 9:40 p.m. They were convinced that Hill's confession was bona fide, and they found him guilty. But they recommended mercy.

Hill entered the New Jersey State Penitentiary in December 1944, and, according to him, he kept his "mind active to avoid dwelling morbidly on a miscarriage of justice." He learned several skills, including the pasteurization of milk.

The world changed . . . The war ended. Dreary Duck Island— used as the setting for a mystery novel, *Halfway House,* by Ellery Queen—lost its lure as a petters' paradise when a huge power station was erected there.

Most important of all, the attitude toward forced confessions underwent change.

Along about 1953, Leon Josephson, a retired New York attorney, became interested in Hill and his story of police brutality. Why, wondered Josephson, was Hill questioned for 34 days before he was arraigned? Why was his case not appealed to a higher court?"

The answer to the second question lay in the fact that Hill had no money to pay for necessary reprints of trial transcript. (Nowadays, and under present procedure, the county pays the printing bill when the convict cannot.)

Josephson and representatives of the American Civil Liberties Union knew that Hill would be eligible for parole in 1959, once he had completed 14 years of servitude at hard labor. Josephson helped the prisoner with a petition for parole, which was presented to the New Jersey State Parole Board in February 1959.

The board refused parole then and rejected petitions presented in '60, '61, and '62. The ACLU sought clemency for Hill on the ground that his confession was forced by pressure and community hysteria.

In 1963, about the time Hill, a model prisoner, was transferred to Leesburg Prison Farm near Maurice River, N.J., the board again took up the question of his parole.

By this time, Mercer County was willing to drop the five indictments remaining against Hill, "because two key witnesses have died and the confession Hill made couldn't be admitted in court as evidence under present standards forbidding coercion." (This was a tacit admission that Hill was beaten in Hamilton Township.)

But the most compelling reason for the board's decision to parole Hill was that he had throat cancer.

A cousin, a sister and Josephson were at the prison farm to greet him the morning of April 24, 1964. The hour of his release was set for 9:30 a.m. At 9 o'clock, the prison's chief deputy, Arthur Edmonds, received a telephone call. Bucks County authorities asked that Hill be held as a fugitive from the 1944 indictments relating to the two attacks made on couples in Pennsylvania.

So Hill left prison in handcuffs. He was taken directly to a magistrate's court in Trenton for a hearing on the fugitive warrant. Then he was ordered to Mercer County Jail to await the extradition procedure which would take him to Pennsylvania.

However, on the plea of Hill's lawyers, County Judge Clifton C. Bennett granted him liberty on $10,000 bail so he could be taken to a New York hospital for cobalt treatments that might stem the spread of his disease. (The bail was raised on a piece of land inherited by Hill and his sister, Lizzie Short, while he was in prison.)

"I'm glad to be out," said Hill, "and I thank all the people who helped me. I never killed any person or persons, and I knew time would rectify the situation."

Last August, Hill became a really free man when New Jersey's Gov. Richard J. Hughes refused to grant Pennsylvania's request to extradite.

What is justified in the Hill case? Did he actually kill six people on Duck Island, terrify three Pennsylvanians and force another to go through life with one arm? Or was he caught in the long arm of coincidence and then beaten into a false confession?

The Dutch Freighter Affair

JOSEPH MCNAMARA
NOVEMBER 4, 1984

Thirteen hours after word was radioed that vivacious Lynn Kauffman had vanished from the Dutch freighter *Utrecht* under steam in Boston Harbor, her partially nude body was spied in the surf off nearby Spectacle Island. That was 1:30 p.m. Saturday, Sept. 19, 1959—about the time the *Utrecht* berthed at Bush Terminal, Brooklyn, to end a 33-day voyage from Singapore.

How the shapely 23-year-old brunet divorcée disappeared from the ship, how she mysteriously met her death in the harbor waters and the tantalizing "why?" were questions that were soon to snag the rapt attention of two continents.

Lynn was the pretty secretary, research assistant and translator of Stanley Spector, Far East studies professor at Washington University in St. Louis. She had just spent a year with him and his family in the Orient, on a grant to help him research a book.

On the long voyage home, Mrs. Kauffman—she used the "Mrs." with her maiden name—was a delight to her eight fellow passengers. She amused the dozen Dutch officers and captivated Chinese and Vietnamese seamen with small talk in their native tongues. Just the night before she disappeared, she had given a birthday party for Spector's wife, Juanita, who made the passage with the three Spector children and a 15-year-old Chinese youth the Spectors were adopting. The professor had flown home nine days before. All that morning of Sept. 18, however, Lynn languished with a migraine in her cabin, No. 7, resisting entreaties to come to lunch and dinner.

At 6:55 p.m., when the *Utrecht* was passing Spectacle Island, Kauffman begged off Juanita Spector's tap on the door. At 7:02 p.m., on a "last call," she told second steward Lubertus Van Dorp through her closed door, "I don't feel well enough to go to dinner." Van Dorp said later that her voice was trembling.

At 9 p.m. the door of Cabin 7 was forced open, and the room was found to be empty, both portholes wide open. A search of the ship followed, and the radio alert went out to the Coast Guard at 12:22 a.m.

When the body of the 95-pound Lynn Kauffman was removed from the water, it was clad only in gray Bermuda shorts and blue terry-cloth slippers. An autopsy found death by drowning, but there were immediate suspicions of murder.

Capt. Joseph Fallon of Boston's homicide squad flew to New York City and interviewed the ship's crew and passengers. Back in Boston, Fallon expressed the "belief" that Lynn had committed suicide over "some distressing news she received the day she disappeared." He refused to divulge the news, but said, "It would have affected her life radically."

But Suffolk County (Boston) medical examiner Michael Luongo protested, "I'm not buying this suicide idea at all. This girl died of drowning after violence. She had been so badly kicked and pummeled, she was incapable of moving voluntarily into the water." Luongo added that there were 27 bruises on the body, two skull fractures—one on each side of the head—which caused brain hemorrhage, two black eyes.

Professor Spector insisted, "Lynn must have been murdered— she was a brilliant woman, not the suicidal type." Her Chicago manufacturer father agreed. Spector denied a report that Lynn was to be forced out of her room in the Spector home to make way for the adopted Chinese youth, apparently the "news" that Fallon referred to. In fact, said Spector, he was painting her room when he got word of her death.

Meanwhile, Brooklyn detectives learned from several crew members that Lynn had spent some nights of the long voyage in the cabin of tall, handsome radio operator Willem Van Rie, 30. Van Rie, of the wavy hair and blue-gray eyes, had told Detective Lt. Victor Kaufman earlier that he had never spent more than 10 minutes alone with Lynn. He had married just before putting to sea.

Detectives had wondered why Van Rie's coat was found in Kauffman's cabin. Or why there were erasures and inaccuracies in his log, as his captain indicated. Or where he was between 7 and

7:30 p.m., when police figured Lynn went over the side. Van Rie
was off duty between 7 and 9 p.m.

Alerted on Sept. 30 by Brooklyn detectives of new evidence,
Fallon returned and, with local sleuths, questioned Van Rie again.
At one point Detective Kaufman asked, "What was Lynn Kauffman's
lipstick doing on your pillowcase?"

Rattled, the Dutch national assertedly replied, "I didn't think
you would find me out." He then told this story:

Nine days out of Singapore, Lynn asked him if he liked sleeping alone, and when he said no, offered to visit his cabin. There
were many trysts after that, the last one from 1 a.m. to 4 a.m., Sept.
18, her last day on board, Van Rie revealed. He had denied having
sex with her to save his job, he said.

Asked if Mrs. Kauffman could have taken her own life because
of pregnancy, Van Rie replied that she had a contraceptive device.
(The autopsy confirmed she was not pregnant.) Pressed about a
possible suicide because Lynn found out he was married, Van Rie
said, "No, she was interested in someone else. I made no secret of
my marriage."

Just before 6:00 that morning, Van Rie made a statement. He
said that about 7 p.m. on Sept. 18, he visited Lynn in her cabin. She
was wearing only the shorts and slippers she was later found dead
in. She said she was still sick.

"What's the matter—are you pregnant?" he asked.

"What would you do if I were?" she snapped. Van Rie laughed.
Lynn flew at him in a rage and he became furious.

"I beat her unmercifully," the radio man confessed. "I beat her
with my left, I beat her with my right. She fell to the floor. I threw
her into the bunk. I heard a knock on her door and told her to

reply. She said through the door she was too sick to go to dinner. I then left her sobbing."

Van Rie was returned to Boston, but almost immediately retracted his statement, except for the love trysts. A grand jury in Suffolk County indicted him for first-degree murder, setting the stage for a trial watched as closely in Van Rie's native Rijen, Holland, as in Massachusetts. When the trial began on Feb. 10, 1960, before Judge Frank Murray and an all-male jury, five Netherlands newspapers were represented. The country's consul to Boston attended daily. Assistant District Attorney John McAuliffe insisted that Van Rie beat Lynn fiercely, shoved her out a porthole over her bed and hurled her into the water to conceal his guilty sexual dalliance with the sophisticated beauty.

Luongo, the medical examiner, testified that Lynn's injuries were consistent with a beating by fists and being shoved out the porthole and falling to the deck, before she was hurled overboard.

To rebut defense allegations of suicide, Juanita Spector testified she and Lynn had "disagreements," but denied they had quarreled. She told of the birthday party Lynn gave her the night before she died. At that party, a passenger testified, Lynn had worn Van Rie's coat, which came down to the slits in her Oriental dress.

"Lynn, change your clothes," Van Rie had laughed, according to the witness. "You give me naughty thoughts."

Van Rie took the stand and made these points: Lynn often did sewing for the ship's officers and that's why his coat was in her cabin. Between 7 and 7:30 p.m., when she disappeared, he was mostly in the radio room.

The accused swore that the last time he saw Lynn was at customs in the lounge at 8 a.m. that morning, that he last spoke to her at noon through the porthole of her cabin. He denied that he ever beat the woman and insisted he was forced to make his statement during all-night questioning.

He admitted under cross-examination by McAuliffe that he had spent seven or eight nights with Lynn in his cabin. He also admitted he had lied many times, but only to save his job.

The defense then sprang the prestigious Dr. Milton Helpern, chief medical examiner of New York. He testified that Lynn's injuries were not caused by a beating with fists, but rather by the body's bouncing on the folded gangplank on its way into the water. Other injuries were caused, he believed, when the body struck the water at 35 miles an hour.

Under Massachusetts law, the defendant can make a final statement. Said Van Rie: "I have committed the sin of adultery with Lynn Kauffman and I know it was wrong. My wife has forgiven me of punishment for this sin."

He looked across the courtroom at his dark-haired seamstress wife, Nella, here for the trial.

"But I never kicked nor hit nor beat Mrs. Kauffman. I never committed that sin. I never pushed her overboard," he concluded.

The jury took 20 ballots; the first deadlocked at 6-6. After 15 hours, foreman Charles Carroll read the verdict: Not guilty.

Van Rie returned to the Netherlands, forsook the sea, went to work for a publishing house and began to raise a family. On Sept. 12, 1961, Professor Spector was granted a divorce from Juanita for "general indignities," a catchall charge in Missouri marital suits. One complaint was that his wife "made false accusations with regard to his association with other women."

A Crime Accented in Red

JOSEPH MCNAMARA
OCTOBER 6, 1985

It did not take detectives long to call them the Red Circle Murders, the mysterious slayings of a young man and his sweetheart in a desolate lovers' lane in Hollis Woods, Queens. Ten newspapers, vying for circulation and the Depression-era dollar of 1937, eagerly reported every grisly detail. The moniker came easily. The killer, in what passes for reasoning in the homicidal mind, had decided to draw a circle of red on the forehead of each victim, using the slain woman's lipstick.

What an avenue of possibilities these scarlet symbols opened to students of the occult and the weird. Young lovers were terrified.

The victims, ambushed during a woodland tryst in Queens Village, had been shot twice each in the right temple with a .25-caliber automatic. The woman, blond and pretty Frances Hajek, 19, had also been stabbed seven times in the chest with a narrow blade, possibly an ice pick. She was an only child, under strict parental restraint. She helped by day in the family bakery on Jamaica Ave. in Queens Village, where she also lived. At night she studied dress design at Pratt Institute.

Not formally engaged, she had "an understanding" of marriage with Lewis Weiss, 20, of Queens Village, also an only child. He was a clerk at a Manhattan steel and wire firm and studied civil engineering at Cooper Union at night. The son of a wholesale grocery salesman, Weiss had been a star athlete at Jamaica High School.

His body was found behind the wheel of his coupe in a clearing of young oaks and maples off Grand Central Parkway. In his lap lay his wallet, opened to his driver's license. Next to him was the body of Frances, her red velvet dress askew up over her thighs as her torso had slid half out of the car, the door apparently having been wrenched open by the killer. Her right leg was on the ground, her left on the car floor.

Three .25-caliber shell casings were found, two on the floor of the auto, one underneath it. The fourth was missing. But the couple's jewelry was intact; a gold cross on a chain around Frances' neck, a Jamaica High ring on one finger, a white gold ring with two diamonds and a sapphire on another. Weiss wore a signet ring. His watch had a shattered crystal, its hands stopped at 2:42.

A horrified hiker found the bodies at 1:30 p.m. Sunday, Oct. 3, 1937, and immediately notified police. Though concerned that the couple had not returned from their roller-skating date the night before, both families had not ruled out elopement.

Assistant Medical Examiner Howard W. Neail performed an autopsy, which determined the woman had not been assaulted and that she was a virgin. About the frenzied stabbings after Hajek was already dead from the bullet wounds, Dr. Neail declared: "It is my theory that Weiss died an accidental victim of some hatred born of jealousy that some individual had for Miss Hajek."

Hajek's parents, Frank and Anna Hajek, who had immigrated here from Hungary 22 years before, could not reconcile their daughter's peaceful life with a vengeance motive. They said Weiss, whom she had known since childhood and loved for 18 months, was the only boyfriend she ever had.

The father did, however, tell detectives about a determined suitor who "wrote her crazy poetry."

"He followed her to and from church and waited for her on the steps," Frank Hajek told cops." He used to come into my bakery and try to date her. She never would have anything to do with him."

The "Mad Poet," as headline writers dubbed him, was picked up for questioning—and released.

Creedmoor State Hospital for the Insane, about a mile from the murder scene, was checked. No inmate had escaped. Two attendants—one with scratches on his face—were quizzed. Both were exonerated.

The coupe was dusted for fingerprints, but no useful ones were found.

Most puzzling were the red circles left by the killer. Some investigators thought them the work of an adolescent whose mind was filled with cheap mystery tales. Although the circle symbol dates back to pagan times and has meant many things to many people, investigators believed them a sudden afterthought of the murderer. If not, they reasoned, the killer would have brought his own marker instead of using the victim's lipstick, which lab workers had proved was indeed the case.

Neail pointed out that Hajek's lipstick was not smudged and there was no lipstick on Weiss, indicating to him that the couple had not kissed and were killed as soon as the car stopped. Was the killer lurking in the woods, a popular spot for lovers and, by day, picnickers? Had he approached the car as it turned off Grand Central Parkway and, at gunpoint, forced Weiss to drive further up the lane? Or had he met them outside the Mineola Skating Rink, where they had been, or some other spot? Indeed, was the killer a man?

Raymond J. Burns, head of the Burns Detective Agency, in a series of articles for the *Daily News,* saw the killer as a vengeful woman.

"Women slayers, as a rule, are far more vicious than men, particularly when dealing with their rivals," he wrote.

Twenty-year-old Lewis Weiss, branded on his forehead with a circle of red lipstick, was found dead behind the wheel of his car shortly after he and his girlfriend, Frances Hajek—also mortally wounded—parked in a remote area in Queens. Both were victims during a homicidal spree in 1937 called the Red Circle Murders. The perpetrator was never caught.

Honest, reliable, kindly, willing and, above all, truthful was the way neighbors described mama's boy Ed Gein. Gein's macabre "hobby" inspired Alfred Hitchcock's movie *Psycho*.

AP/Wide World Photos

The gruesome murder of Elizabeth Short—nicknamed "The Black Dahlia"—spawned more bogus admissions of guilt than any other case in California history. More than 40 people confessed to the notorious crime, including the author of this letter cut from newspapers and pasted on an envelope. Inside the envelope were Short's birth certificate, address book, social security card, and some personal belongings. The real killer was never found.

Lizzie Borden hardly looked like a brutal ax murderer. The Fall River, Mass., jury agreed and found her not guilty of the bloody slayings of her father and stepmother.

THIS IS LIZZIE AT THE AGE OF 29

"Lizzie Borden took an ax
And gave her mother forty whacks;
When she saw what she had done
She gave her father forty-one!"

In what was labeled "The Trial of the Century," Bruno Richard Hauptmann was found guilty of the kidnaping and murder of Charles Lindbergh Jr. Despite the protestations of many that Hauptmann was innocent, he died in the electric chair in 1936.

WANTED

INFORMATION AS TO THE
WHEREABOUTS OF

CHAS. A. LINDBERGH, Jr.
OF HOPEWELL, N. J.

SON OF COL. CHAS. A. LINDBERGH
World-Famous Aviator

This child was kidnaped from his home
in Hopewell, N. J., between 8 and 10 p. m.
on Tuesday, March 1, 1932.

DESCRIPTION:

Age, 20 months   Hair, blond, curly
Weight, 27 to 30 lbs.   Eyes, dark blue
Height, 29 inches   Complexion, light
Deep dimple in center of chin
Dressed in one-piece coverall night suit

ADDRESS ALL COMMUNICATIONS TO
COL. H. N. SCHWARZKOPF, TRENTON, N. J., or
COL. CHAS. A. LINDBERGH, HOPEWELL, N. J.

ALL COMMUNICATIONS WILL BE TREATED IN CONFIDENCE

COL. H. NORMAN SCHWARZKOPF
March 11, 1932   Supt. New Jersey State Police, Trenton, N. J.

The police circular issued by Col. H. Norman
Schwarzkopf of the New Jersey State Police asks
for information as to the whereabouts of the
Lindbergh baby.

H.R.H. THE LATE DUKE OF CLARENCE AND AVONDALE.

Shown here in his regimentals, the Duke of Clarence was something of a royal dandy referred to on occasion as "Uncle-Eddy-Collars-and-Cuffs." Many scholars and researchers believe this grandson of Queen Victoria was also the notorious butcher of prostitutes, Jack the Ripper.

Fun-loving Regina Ball traded her cocktail lounge job for marriage to a millionaire builder from a high-society Miami family. The fun stopped shortly after the marriage and eventually erupted in a gun battle that killed Regina and her lover. Regina's wealthy husband, Robert Ball, was found guilty of the killings and sentenced to two life terms in prison.

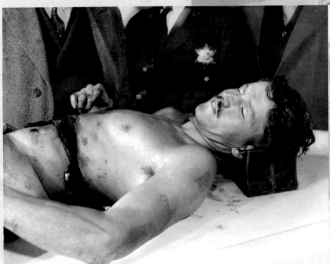

The bullet-riddled body of Baby Face Nelson lies on a slab in a San Francisco morgue. At the time, the trigger-happy gangster was the FBI's Public Enemy No. 1.

"Candelight Killer" Robert Liberty waves to spectators after he and his girlfriend, Kendall Bierly, who later became his bride, were caught by a lone detective in a 100 mph car chase in Colorado Springs, Colo. While awaiting trial in a San Diego jail, Liberty was strangled by fellow inmates who believed, wrongly, that Liberty was a police informant.

Richard "Peg Leg" Lonergan lived the good life—until he was murdered. The leader of the White Hands gang—the Irish answer to the Italians' Black Hands—Lonergan met his end at the hands of Al Capone.

Manhattan gambler and notorious playboy Joseph Elwell is shown here enjoying the carefree lifestyle of Palm Beach, Fla. However, after his return to New York City, Elwell was found mortally wounded in his lavish Manhattan home. His mysterious death was the subject of the first weekly "Justice" feature in the *Daily News,* appearing on May 6, 1923, under the headline "What Has Happened to Justice?"

There was no shortage of theories. Police Commissioner Lewis Valentine was convinced the killer was a sadist. Assistant Chief Inspector John Lyons thought him a bushwhacker who spied on petting parties. Deputy Chief Inspector John Ryan felt he may have posed as a cop, and Weiss was showing him his driver's license when the shooting began.

From Neail: Vengeance was the motive; the killer was recognized by his victims. Assistant DA Edmund Rowan labeled the murderer "an egomaniac with a flair for the dramatic." Lt. James Smith saw the killer as a neighborhood youth who read lurid sex and adventure stories heavy on symbols.

Seventy-five detectives ran down leads. A youth who had asked Hajek for a date that Saturday night proved he was home asleep when the slayings occurred. A Brooklyn barkeep reported a suspicious man with a cop's shield, muddy shoes and a scratch over one eye—but sleuths could not find him. One "witness" was arrested for giving false information. A Work Projects Administration watchman whose name started with "P" was cited in several letters to police. Four indignant government workers whose last initial was "P" denied hotly that they were involved. A 20-year-old counterman surrendered because he "thought" he might be the right man. He was not.

In reconstructing the fateful date that Saturday night, investigators learned that Weiss picked up Hajek at her home at 7:30 and went to the Mineola Skating Rink. There, they were seen by friends. The couple left at 10:30.

If they met death at 2:42, as Weiss' smashed watch indicated, there were several hours unaccounted for. Postmortem tests supplied a partial answer. Dr. Alexander Gettler, city toxicologist, revealed a shocker in view of insistence by their peers that Weiss and Hajek never drank. Gettler reported that both had alcohol in their systems, much of it undigested, indicating they had imbibed shortly before they were murdered. The stomach contents indicated beer.

There were reports the couple had been seen in two bars in Queens, in the company of several men, near midnight—but the investigators never proved this to their satisfaction.

Police were reasonably sure the killer whipped open the car door, shot Hajek, then Weiss; that in applying the lipstick circles, he noticed some post-death muscle movement in the woman and, finding his gun empty, stabbed her repeatedly. The force of the blows dislodged her body from the car seat.

The missing hours might have provided the clue to trip up the killer, who was never caught. Predictions by psychiatrists of the day that the Red Circle murderer would strike again proved wrong— unless he thereafter struck without the crimson symbols that had terrified Queens.

The Hell-Raising Benders of Kansas

JOSEPH MCNAMARA
SEPTEMBER 22, 1985

Even by the standards of their own place and time—Kansas in the early 1870s—the four members of the Bender family were a singular lot. They have been called the most murderous family in American history, plying their deadly art in a log cabin which served as a general store and inn for weary travelers.

When they suddenly vanished on a spring day in 1873, they created one of the great unsolved mysteries in crime.

There was Pa, John Bender, about 60 when the family arrived in 1870, who claimed to be a Hollander, but the heavy Teutonic tones of his paltry English convinced neighbors he was German. Rawboned and only 5-foot-9, the patriarch of the Hell Benders, as they came to be known, wore a grizzled beard. He said he was a baker.

Ma was about 55, blue-eyed and stocky, and her few English phrases left no doubt about her German ancestry. Her name was Kate, but no one ever called her anything but Ma. Son John Jr. was 27, mustached, slightly built—with an even slighter brain—and spoke English with a guttural accent.

And then there was daughter Kate . . . and she was something else. Red-haired with dark eyes and what was described at the time as "a fine buxom figure," Kate was 24, articulate, a bit saucy. She was a good dancer, rode a horse well and, according to a local newspaper, had "a tigerish grace and animal attraction."

Kate became noted for her beauty, which she put to good account as a lecturer on spiritualism throughout the region. She called herself "Professor Miss Kate Bender" in her advertisements, which modestly proclaimed her ability to "heal diseases, cure blindness, fits and deafness."

The Bender homestead squatted near the road along Drum Creek, seven miles northeast of Cherryvale and 10 miles south of Thayer in Labette County. Built in the spring of 1872 by Pa and his son, it was 20 feet long and 16 feet wide and was divided into two rooms by a hanging canvas from their covered wagon. In front was the public area, a few grocery items for sale and a table to serve meals to the weary traveler. Behind the curtain were living quarters, where overnight guests also slept.

It was spitefully reported that for an extra stipend to Pa, the traveler could share Kate's bed. This might have been so, but no one ever lived to brag about it.

That summer a traveler was found dead in Drum Creek with his head crushed and his throat slit. A bit later another body with the same injuries was found in a cottonwood thicket along the creek. A meeting of settlers was called to discuss the matter. Bender and his son attended. Nothing was resolved, but no more bodies were found. Instead, travelers began to disappear.

There were W.F. McCrotty and Benjamin Brown, seeking homesteads on government land with $3,000 between them; H.F. McKegzie and John Creary, owners of handsome carriages which vanished also; G.W. Lauchor and daughter, age five.

At noon on March 10, 1873, Dr. William H. York, a prominent physician from Independence, Kan., 14 miles to the west, stopped at the cabin for lunch. He had told his brother, Col. A.M. York at Ft. Scott, whom he had visited, that he would do so. The doctor promptly vanished.

A month later, two men stopped for lunch. They were L.T. Stephenson of Independence, treasurer of Montgomery County, and District Judge H.G. Webb of Parsons. The new buggy with sparkling bays carrying silver-mounted harness was turned over to the churlish Bender.

"Feed the horses, but don't unhitch them," Stephenson told Bender. "The judge and I have to get on to Parsons." Inside, the two men met a handsome woman dressed in black.

"I am Kate and I will prepare your meal," she said, directing them to seats at a table with their backs to the canvas wall. While Kate labored over the food in the back, the fidgety Stephenson went to inspect the horses. He was incensed to find them in stalls in the locked barn.

While he explained this to Judge Webb, Kate entered with the food and said, "Draw up." Then she retired. With a single move, both men shifted their plates to opposite ends of the table. Suddenly, a heavy object bashed the canvas where their heads had been momentarily before.

Thoroughly shocked, both men drew pistols and backed out of the tavern. Stephenson shot the lock off the barn door and hitched his team. They sped off in a cloud of dust.

In telling their story at home, they learned of other dark tales on Drum Creek. They heard about a fellow named Corlew who heard moans from the kitchen of the Benders' cabin and was assured by the soothing Kate that a hog had fallen through a trapdoor to the cellar and injured itself.

Corlew offered to help and was assaulted by Pa in fractured English, "None your business . . . No like, get the hell out!" Corlew did, fast.

They learned of Happy Jack Reed of Independence, who vowed that when he arrived for supper, Kate wore a fetching smile—and little else. This interesting episode ended abruptly, however, with the untimely arrival of other diners. He did return the next night, though, at Kate's urging. Reed said he paid Pa the little extra and things hummed along nicely—until two friends of his dropped by and Reed told them to inform his relatives where he was spending the night.

"Kate turned cold," Reed reported later, and he went to bed alone. At midnight he heard blows and screams from the stable and Kate hovered over his bed as he feigned sleep.

"You hear anything last night?" Kate asked him in the morning. "No," he lied, and promptly left.

Meanwhile, Col. York had been searching for his brother. York heard of Stephenson's experience at the Benders' and sought him out. Accompanied by several men, they rode to the log cabin May 1. "Your brother had dinner here and then rode west," Kate told York.

The posse searched about. Pa and his son helped drag Drum Creek. "We'll ride on," York told the Benders, "but if we don't find my brother, we'll be back."

When they returned, on May 5, the Benders were gone. What the searchers found sickened them. An overpowering stench led them to a trapdoor at the rear of the cabin. It opened to a six-foot cubed pit, slick with human blood.

"Look on the prairie," York ordered. And suspicious mounds, partially concealed by plowing, were excavated. The first yielded the body of Dr. York. In other graves were McCrotty, Brown, McKegzie, Creary, Lauchor and his daughter. All had crushed heads and slit throats, except the girl, who had been strangled.

Eleven bodies were found. Locals theorized that the probable number of victims ranged as high as 104, but it was more likely 15.

The modus operandi of the Hell Benders was clear: Strangers would be induced to sit by the much-washed canvas, and Pa or son would crush their heads with a hammer. Then the victim would be held over the pit, his neck slit, and the body dumped in. At nightfall he would be buried on the prairie. Clothing, horses and saddles were apparently sold to "fences" in the nearby Indian territory, now Oklahoma.

A team and wagon were located near a rail line that might have been an escape route to Texas. The governor offered a $500 reward for their capture, but it was never collected.

Rumors were rife. One had the Benders executed by a posse and Kate defiantly shouting, "Shoot and be damned!" Two posse members, on their deathbeds years later, said the Benders were dumped into a well, the men sworn to secrecy. But the site described turned out to be a plowed cornfield with no well.

For years, the Benders were "sighted" throughout the west. But as W.E. Connelley, secretary of the Kansas State Historical Society, noted in the 1950s, "there is no proof for any statement concerning the Benders after their disappearance."

Hollywood Homicide

Joseph McNamara
March 8, 1998

Three neighbors heard the shot that claimed the life of storied silent film director William Desmond Taylor, but the sound reverberated through the entire movie industry and a nation that hung on its every word and deed.

Ironically, the shot sounded enough like an auto backfire that the neighbors did nothing about it. It was not until the next morning, Feb. 2, 1922, at 7:30 that valet Henry Peavey found the handsome 45-year-old director dead on his back in his Los Angeles living room.

Taylor appeared peaceful, feet together, hands at his side, his suit jacket buttoned, just a trickle of dried blood from his mouth. The high-living filmmaker seemed to have had a heart attack, until emergency personnel turned him over—and found a .38-caliber wound in his back.

The slaying had all the story qualities a director would want: mystery, love, hate, money, famed actresses, alluring women, narcotics addicts and ruined reputations. If anything, it might be too grotesque and bizarre for fiction.

Hollywood was still rocking from allegations that Roscoe "Fatty" Arbuckle had fatally injured actress Virginia Rappe, 25, during a sex bout in his hotel suite. Rappe died of a burst bladder. The 300-pound comic, second in the business only to Charlie Chaplin, was acquitted of manslaughter . . . but his career was over.

And booze and morphine were ending the career of handsome silent star Wallace "Wally" Reid.

Just a week before Taylor met his Maker, Will Hays, postmaster general to President Warren Harding, had taken over as morals czar of the film industry.

In addition to his charm and good looks, lover-boy Taylor had a dash of adventure, an element of mystery, a touch of class.

A little before 7 that fateful night, Mabel Normand, 27, one of Hollywood's best-known comediennes and the director's current love, dropped in after his phoned invite to pick up two books he had for her. Taylor lived in a two-story white stucco cottage at 404-B S. Alvarado St.

Normand found him working on his income tax—income $37,000, tax 4 percent—and grumbling that his former valet, a mysterious Edward Sands, had forged so many checks of Taylor's so expertly before bugging out that the director could not make out the forgeries from the genuine.

While Taylor was in England, Sands used his employer's credit, pawned his jewelry, stole most of his clothes, wrecked two of his cars and slipped away. Later came the forgeries and two burglaries.

As Taylor spoke, someone—possibly Sands, maybe Taylor's killer—stood outside the back door and smoked cigarette after cigarette. Cops later found a neat little pile of butts at the spot. Whoever he was, he was not seen by Peavey when the new valet left at 7:30 p.m. (None of Taylor's servants slept in.)

At 7:45, Taylor saw Normand to her car on the street, promised to call her at 9 p.m. and returned to his house. A neighbor, Faith Cole MacLean, saw the leave-taking and Taylor's return to his house.

Half an hour later, MacLean's husband, actor Douglas MacLean, and two other neighbors heard the shot. No one looked out, but Faith did have a peek later. She saw a man leave Taylor's house through an alley next to the garage.

"He walked like a woman and had the build of a woman," she would say later. The figure wore a cap and a mackinaw with heavy muffler about his face.

"It wasn't Sands," said MacLean. "I know him."

Poor Peavey, finding his master dead, gave a piercing scream. One neighbor, Edna Purviance, Chaplin's leading lady, heard him. This would explain why Purviance the night before got no answer when she knocked at Taylor's door.

Purviance quickly phoned Normand, who almost collapsed at the news. She also called Mary Miles Minter, the curly blond ingenue who was being mentioned as a replacement for Mary Pickford. Minter was not home, so Purviance left word with Minter's mother, Charlotte Shelby.

"Mr. Taylor was found murdered this morning," Shelby told her daughter when she arrived home, adding tactfully, "Where were you last night?"

Minter rushed to Alvarado St. in hysterics. As near as could be determined at the time, she was wildly in love with Taylor, who was ecstatic over the vivacious Normand.

"Bill, my darling, speak to me," Minter screamed as she tried to get through a cordon of police at Taylor's door. After trampling the flower beds, she was induced to leave.

Minter presented herself as 16 and said she and Taylor were engaged to marry when she was 18. Actually, she was about 20 and the engagement probably would have been news to Taylor, who had directed her recently in *Anne of Green Gables*.

Word spread quickly to the Famous Players-Lasy Studio, which employed Taylor, and executives descended on Alvarado St. to "protect" the director's image. They toted off a cache of booze. But cops arrived too soon for them to remove ladies' lingerie, some monogrammed MMM, and other dainties, plus love letters from Minter found in Taylor's boot.

But the protectors managed to stomp on any clues to the killer that might have been there. Robbery did not seem to be a factor. Taylor wore his two-carat diamond ring and platinum wristwatch and had $78 in his pocket.

The colorful director was known as William Desmond Taylor, but he was born William Cunningham "Pete" Deane-Tanner in County Cork, Ireland. His British Army major father wanted him in the military, but poor eyesight precluded this. The family moved to Dublin, and Taylor got a good education.

When Taylor showed an interest in the theater, the old man shipped him off to a ranch in Kansas with his younger brother Dennis. Eventually, Taylor wound up in New York and married Ethel May Harrison. In 1903, they had a daughter, Ethel Daisy. Taylor and his brother ran an antiques shop on Fifth Ave.

On Oct. 23, 1908, Taylor put on his coat and went to lunch. He never came back to the shop, or his home. In 1912, his wife got a divorce on a hotel clerk's testimony that her hubby trysted with a woman for a week in the Adirondacks.

A few years later, she and her daughter saw a handsome actor on the silent screen and she told the girl, "That's your daddy." The program listed him as William Desmond Taylor. In between there had been a little gold prospecting in Colorado and the Klondike.

Taylor soon graduated to directing and made Alvarado St. not only his home but an entertainment mecca for some of Hollywood's most beautiful women.

In fact, the ire of a wronged husband or boyfriend was an initial motive explored by investigators. Another—long held by Los Angeles police—was an underworld hit over Taylor's known fight against narcotics peddlers. Some of his best friends had fallen victim to the dope traffic flourishing in Tinseltown. Taylor gave the law every bit of info he could find about pushers.

For a while, Charlotte Shelby was under suspicion. Her maid told cops Shelby had a .38, practiced with it and had threatened Taylor with it to leave her daughter alone. Shelby denied everything. And daughter Mary Minter swore that mom objected to the liaison "so she could monopolize Taylor's attentions and, if possible, his love."

The cops got nowhere with this angle. Blackmail was a possibility, but again, sleuths found nothing tangible.

Minter, whose screen success was based on the "clean girl next door," skidded right out of films. She never married and died in 1984. Normand went into a slow eclipse and died of tuberculosis in 1930.

To this day, the murder of William Desmond Taylor is as murky, muddled and mysterious as much of his personal life had been.

Mystery Surrounds Fatal Shooting of Hotel Guest

RUTH REYNOLDS
AUGUST 18, 1948

T hree revolver shots rang out.

This fusillade must have sounded like artillery fire in the quiet corridors of the Kenmore, a residential hotel on North Capitol St., in Washington, D.C., at 2 a.m. on May 15, 1901.

Then piteous cries for help came from the fourth floor, Room 20.

Three revolver shots . . . cries for help . . . How often detective fiction writers have used these thrilling properties to launch their stories into action.

But although at least four persons heard the shots and the appeals of a dying man, and in spite of the fact that two of the four saw the flight of a killer, exactly nothing happened. No excitement. No public alarm. No scream of police sirens.

No one—incredible as it may seem—went near the room where 21-year-old John Seymour Ayres Jr. was bleeding away his life for six and a half hours.

A timid little government clerk, Mary Minas, came down the stairs into the hotel lobby at 8:30 a.m. and approached the Kenmore's owner, W.W. Warfield.

"Mr. Warfield, I live in No. 21 on the fourth floor," she began in a whisper.

"Yes?" said proprietor Warfield with raised inflection and eyebrow, both designed to ward off any complaints about the hotel service. Miss Minas gulped and continued:

"I was awakened at 2 o'clock this morning and—and"—she stumbled, uncertain whether she should tell her dread news—"and I heard two shots fired in Room 20, which is next to mine and—and—I also heard someone call for help?"

There! She had told it, and the change on Warfield's countenance repaid her for her previous fear.

Warfield beckoned to one of the waiters, who hurried forward as Mary Minas continued:

"That's Mr. Ayres' room. He's a clerk in the Census Bureau like I am, and he's also a dental student, and—" But Warfield had no time to listen.

"Dan," he said to the waiter, "you go up to No. 20 and see what's going on."

The waiter, hurrying to obey, knocked on Ayres' door, received no answer and then peeped through the keyhole. What he saw made him run back to the lobby crying:

"Mr. Warfield! Oh! Mr. Warfield! Young Mr. Ayres cut his throat. He's lyin' in his own blood without hardly any clothes on!"

"Dan! You shouldn't say things like that!" reprimanded the proprietor sternly. "Shh, lower your voice!"

Jealous for the reputation of his hostelry, Warfield looked to see if the excited waiter had been overheard.

Flanked by his brother and two employees, the proprietor went up to the fourth floor. They, too, pounded the door and then peered through the keyhole. One glance and they understood well the cause of the waiter's shock.

"Bring me a ladder," Warfield ordered.

When the ladder was brought, he ascended, looked over the transom, nodded solemnly and announced to the watchers below:

"I believe we shall have to call the police."

In due time, bluecoats of the District of Columbia police force opened the door with a skeleton key.

The young man's body, clad only in undershirt, trousers and shoes lay in a cramped position on the floor near a window which opened onto a front fire escape. His head rested in a pool of clotted blood.

Ayres' throat was not cut, as reported by the waiter. He had been struck by three bullets—in the left leg, in the left arm, and in the breast in the region of the heart. There were powder burns and scorches on the sleeve and left side of his undershirt.

A Japanese fan, dainty but broken, lay nearby on the floor. On a half-packed trunk lay three empty shells, three unfired cartridges and a pistol. The barrel and trigger of the weapon were smeared with blood, indicating that Ayres, wounded, had grappled with his assailant for the gun. There were bloodstains on the outside wall, as though the slayer had propped himself there for a moment after the murder.

That a battle had preceded Ayres' death was shown by a post-mortem examination. There were bruises on both his legs, bruises which appeared to be the result of strong kicks. There was a slight cut over his nose.

The bullets in the hip and left arm had taken a downward and forward course, indicating that Ayres was lying flat, or nearly so, when they were fired. The bullet which had penetrated the breast had also pierced the left lung, severed one of the main arteries and finally landed against a rib, which was slightly fractured. Ayres, the doctors were sure, actually bled to death when his cries for help went unanswered by the 100 or so people in the Kenmore.

Naturally, the news of the murder spread like plague through the hotel and threw the guests into an uproar.

Some, with more sentiment than others, pointed out that Ayres had said he feared he might fail in his dental examinations, and they declared he had broken under his anxiety and had taken his own life. Others were equally convinced that the handsome young man, well known to be a ladies' man, had met his death at the hands of a wronged woman or a jealous male.

The victim, scion of a prosperous and politically prominent Port Austin, Mich., family, had lived in Washington for 11 months.

He had, as Miss Minas had said, combined the study of dentistry with work as a clerk in the Census Bureau. He was appointed to the job after passing his civil service tests. He had been recommended by Rep. Edgar Weeks, a Republican from Michigan and a friend of his father. Young Ayres was paying marked attention to the representative's pretty debutante daughter.

He was paying equally ardent court to several other ladies, married and single, in his office and in his hotel.

These facts alone were enough to prompt the chief of police to assign eight detectives to the case. It was their task to check Ayres' habits with his friends, to check their alibis, and to check his movements during the hours preceding his death. All this appeared not too difficult, up to a point.

Ayres had returned to the Kenmore immediately after office hours, had dined as usual in the hotel dining room and had then attended a dancing party in one of the hotel parlors.

The party broke up at 10:30. Ayres and three male friends repaired to a nearby tavern for cigars and beers. With James Burns, a close friend, he returned to the hotel at 12:30 a.m. They stopped to chat briefly with another hotel guest, J.V. Wiggins. Then Burns left Ayres at the door of No. 20.

Ayres apparently did not retire at once, for he was seen in the lobby at 1 a.m. He was cheerful and sober as he said goodbye to several loungers here, explaining that he planned to move the next day to a clubhouse on L St.

"You know, that's a strange thing," Burns mused. "John planned several times to move from the Kenmore, but each time he changed his mind and stayed on. And this time, when he had all his arrangements made and his trunk almost packed, he was stopped from leaving."

Presently the police were to ponder with Burns upon that fact, but for the moment they were occupied with their attempt to learn what Ayres did during the 60 minutes between 1 and 2 a.m. They drew a blank.

At 2 o'clock things happened, according to Minas, who was now given her chance to talk.

"About 2 a.m.," she said, "I heard shots and thought at first the sound was in the hallway. I changed my mind shortly afterward and concluded that the trouble had occurred in Mr. Ayres' room. That was when I heard someone call, 'Help! Help!'

"Then he groaned and cried piteously for five or 10 minutes. That somebody had been killed I felt certain."

Minas added that from the time she heard the cries until 6 a.m. she walked the floor of her room. Then she opened her door quietly, peeped out cautiously "and I was surprised when I failed to find the body of a burglar in the hall."

"Why on earth didn't you press the electric call bell in your room?" asked Lola Bonine, the hotel hostess, who also lived on the fourth floor.

"Why, I don't know—I just didn't think of it," answered the frightened Minas.

"It is certainly strange that Minas heard so much," snapped Kate Lawless, another fourth-floor guest. "I lived right next to Ayres on the north, and my room is separated from his by only a thin partition and I heard nothing—no shots, no cries, no disturbance."

"Maybe you're a sound sleeper," Minas suggested.

Minas' reputation for veracity was saved by others who had heard the shots and cries.

R.P. Hokins, who occupied a room directly across the inner court from No. 20, said he heard "three shots fired in rapid succession. I left my room to make inquiry, but there was no one about."

Another light sleeper, Thomas M. Baker, who boarded in a house across the street from the Kenmore, leaped from his bed when he heard the shots. Someone on the floor below him was looking out and called up:

"What's wrong?"

"I heard some pistol shots," said Baker.

"So did I," answered his neighbor, who then withdrew.

Baker continued to stand at his window. Some five minutes later his somewhat aimless vigil was rewarded.

"While watching, I saw a form come from a window on the fourth floor and, without hurrying, descend the fire escape to the second floor. I am positive it was a woman in a night robe, with hair hanging. She stepped from the fire escape through a window on the second floor."

The fourth-floor window indicated by Baker was Ayres' room. The second-floor window led to a room then tenantless.

Baker's statement received unexpected corroboration from 14-year-old Willie Wolfe, who also lived across the street from the Kenmore. Willie, the fire buff son of a policeman, was proud of his ability to wake up with every fire alarm at any hour of the night. So it wasn't surprising that he heard the shots.

He reached his window just in time to see the figure—he wasn't positive it was a woman—leave from Ayres' fourth-floor window and descend to the second-floor window.

Now, just why none of these witnesses called the police, or at least the night clerk at the Kenmore, is something which wasn't explained by anyone but Minas. Either they lacked phones, courage, curiosity, or all three.

But the statements of Baker and Willie were enough to convince the gossips, and perhaps the police, that the Ayres killing was a crime of passion. Because of the presence of the broken fan in his room, both police and gossips believed that the nocturnal visitor was a woman.

"I remember he kept asking me to have the broken lock on his room door fixed, saying he didn't want to be pestered," volunteered Warfield.

"Did he say who he wanted to keep out?"

"I didn't ask and I wasn't told," was the smug retort.

Warfield's employees were less discreet.

"I went twice to fix that busted lock," volunteered William Pearce, the hotel's general handyman, "and each time I went there, Mrs. Bonine, the hostess, was looking at his medical books."

Eliza Gardner, a maid, said, "Yes, Mrs. Bonine often came into No. 20 and took a book when I was cleaning and Mr. Ayres wasn't there."

Talk took a new turn and backstairs gossip became lobby rumor.

Said Emma Brown, a nurse employed by one of the guests:

"I saw Mrs. Bonine coming out of Room 20 once with Mr. Ayres one Sunday morning about 10 o'clock. He didn't have no coat or shirt.

"And another time I was in there when Mr. Ayres was washing up and Mrs. Bonine came in.

"He was mad and said, 'Don't come into my room.' Later on she told me, 'He's only mad because he thinks I told people in the hotel that he drinks too much. I never did anything of the kind.'"

Minas knew that Bonine had gone to Ayres' room occasionally at night, and James Burns knew they had quarreled about John's predilection for beer.

He wondered whether Bonine might have been Ayres' reason for not changing residences.

There was so much talk about Bonine that the police assigned Detective Sgt. Edward Horne to look particularly into her alibi, her behavior and her general character.

Lola Bonine, a trim little woman of 34 with a bland smile, told him she worked at the hotel (1) because her husband, Robert, was a traveling salesman and she had time on her hands and (2) because they needed the money.

Lola lived on the fourth floor with her young sons, Maurice and Clesleight, and with her husband when he was in Washington. (He was out of the city at the time of the murder.)

Lola took Detective Horne's shadowing with such good grace that the detective soon joined her in pleasantries. She answered all his questions. She said she had met Ayres soon after he came to the hotel, that she sometimes borrowed his medical books because she had once studied medicine, that she thought well of his character but had once rebuked him for excessive drinking.

"Where did you get that scratch and that bruise on your right hand?" Detective Horne asked her.

"Picking lilacs."

"What skirt did you wear the night of the murder?"

"This one," she answered, looking down at the gray flannel. "Would you like to search my room?"

Detective Horne had already done that.

If Lola took the detective's shadowing with equanimity, her husband, who arrived in Washington two days after the murder, did not.

He was furious at the suspicion against his wife, suspicion which backfired until he offered an impregnable alibi.

He pointed out that Lola, as the hotel hostess, had to be friendly with Ayres, as she was friendly with all the guests. Hadn't she befriended young government clerks, male and female, and gone often to their rooms with tidbits, medicines and books? Was it not true that she had danced with many men as often as she had danced with John?

As for the weapon and fan found in Ayres' room—neither was hers, said Bonine. It was true, her husband said, that Lola knew how to shoot. He had taught her with his own gun. But that gun had been given away some time before.

Bonine's stout defense of his wife failed to lessen the flood of rumors or to discourage Detective Horne, who had questioned her closely more than 20 times.

On Sunday evening, May 19, the detective took her to supper and stopped in the middle of the meal to say calmly:

"Now, my little woman, you know about this affair, and while you can deny it if you like, I wish you would tell me what you know about it."

Pushing her plate back in disgust, Bonine protested, "When will this cease?"

"When we get the woman who murdered that man."

"All right, I may tell you something in the morning. My God, the strain is horrible and my innocence is all that keeps me up!"

The detective had now become a fisherman, and this was his first nibble. He nodded, played out more line, then took Lola back to her hotel.

This fish was caught.

The next morning Lola went voluntarily in search of the detective to tell her story. She said Ayres came to her room shortly before 2 a.m.

"He rapped on the door, and when I opened it, I saw he wasn't dressed; that is, he had no coat nor socks. He wanted to come into my room, but I told him my boys were asleep. He wanted some medicine for a chill, he said.

"Then he asked me to come to his room to talk over the misunderstanding we'd had over his drinking. As he was leaving the hotel in the morning and I wanted no hard feelings, I said I would and that I would bring some medicine.

"I dressed completely and went over.

"When I entered, he was behind the door, and it wasn't until I was fully in that I saw he was only partially dressed and had a pistol in one hand. With the other he closed and bolted the door and said, 'Now, I guess you will listen to me!'"

Bonine said she looked about wildly, and when she realized that the young man was between her and the bolted door she started for the window.

"I wanted to get away without creating alarm. I knew if I made a disturbance at that hour of the night, people would criticize me. I had taken just a few steps when I tripped. He caught me with his left arm about my waist and he wasn't exactly smiling. He was pointing his pistol."

At this point her story followed a familiar pattern: There was a struggle. Both went down. The gun went off. Everything went black.

"The next thing I remember, I was on the fire escape. How I ever got the window open I don't know," she said.

Down the fire escape she went, into the second-story window and through the vacant room to a parlor. There she hid behind a heavy curtain until she knew no one was about. Then she walked back to the fourth floor room where her boys slept.

There she washed the bloodstains from her wrapper and went to bed to await developments. So good a cleaning job had she done that the investigators, searching her room, had found nothing amiss with the garment.

The excitement over Bonine's statement, arrest and eventual indictment died down, and for six months of a sticky Washington summer, she languished, almost forgotten, in a jail cell. She went to trial on Nov. 19. Her defense was that she, like any good woman, was defending her honor against a lustful and determined man.

But the government's case, as outlined by Assistant U.S. Attorney High T. Taggart, painted her as a wanton wife, in love with a lad 13 years her junior, determined he should not get away.

The government's questions were pointed, but its witnesses were not too sure of themselves. There was none to say, for a fact, that Lola ever showed more interest in Ayres than she had in others.

Taggart's theory was that on this last night Ayres was to be in the hotel, Lola took her husband's gun, which they had not given away, as he had told police, and went along the fire escape to Ayres' room. If she had not plotted this murder, how did she know about the tenantless room on the second floor through which she could make her exit?

Ayres, said Taggart, lay on his bed until he was attracted by noise at the open window. Lola was crouching there, and as he rose, she fired. The first shot struck him in the left leg. He rushed toward the window. The second bullet struck him and set his undershirt afire. Still charging, he reached the window, grappled for the gun, and then fell with the third bullet in his heart. Blood spurted from his wounds and stained Bonine's garments.

Why would an innocent woman, one defending her honor, sneak down the fire escape? Why would she hide behind a curtain? Why would she wash her clothes so carefully that all traces of stain were gone?

Why, if innocent of premeditated murder, had she pretended she had no part in the killing until she had that she had ever, had his love, hence none to say she feared losing his love. No one came forth to swear that either the fan or the gun was hers.

The defense made much of these flaws in the government's case. Using the testimony of three witnesses, the defense showed that Ayres brought a gun from Michigan and habitually kept a pistol in his bureau drawer. Expert marksmen showed that the shots, if fired by someone crouching on the fire escape, would hardly have followed the course of the bullets that entered Ayres' body.

The defense lawyers did not minimize Bonine's indiscretion in being in a man's room alone at such an hour, but it made much of her position, pointing out that she was used to ministering to the needs of people and that her heart was generally overflowing with human kindness.

Taggart then changed a few details but, for the most part, stuck to his simple formula:

Lola had gone to Ayres' room, seized the gun from the place she knew he kept it, and shot him.

Summing up for the government, U.S. Attorney Ashley M. Gould asked why Mrs. Bonine hadn't rung the electric call bell when she saw Ayres holding the pistol, even as she had suggested Minas should have done.

"I don't know," thundered Gould, "whether she came up the fire escape, whether she secreted herself in the room or whether Ayres let her in. But I do know that her story is a thing to cause mirth and laughter. If that story will acquit her, then human life in the District of Columbia is not safe against a secret enemy."

The jurors didn't seem to care much about human life in the District of Columbia. They deliberated five hours. They filed back from jury room to courtroom. The verdict: Not guilty.

Mayhem

Desperadoes of the Great Depression haunt this book, the public enemies with household names—the wild purveyors of mayhem. There is John Dillinger, who cut a wide path of crime through the Midwest. And fellow gang member George Nelson, who knew no fear and delighted in killing. He was called Baby Face Nelson, but never in his presence.

Or hoodlum Alvin "Creepy" Karpis, labeled by then-FBI director J. Edgar Hoover "The Rat," with good reason.

You'll meet Sophie Lyons, the stylish queen of con ladies, and Typhoid Mary, who unwittingly spread mayhem throughout New York City. And Virginia Hill, that glamorous doll of the underworld. And more.

A Gem of a Theft

JOSEPH MCNAMARA
JANUARY 23, 1994

One of the boldest thefts of all time was the 1671 swiping of the British crown jewels from the Tower of London, an unthinkable effrontery in today's world of massive security. But just as Abraham Lincoln's life at Ford's Theater was entrusted to a single drunken cop, so were the famed baubles left in charge of a toothless 70-year-old.

The gem thief was Thomas Blood, a most audacious character—patriot and hero to some, rogue and scapegrace to others. All agreed he was a volatile, fearless Irishman, artful and clever. He had a tongue gifted with what Elizabeth I termed "blarney."

Blood had fine forebears. His grandfather was a member of Parliament and his father owned an ironworks. Tom, at 22, was a justice of the peace in his native County Meath. Oliver Cromwell, the commoner then ruling England, raised Blood to the landed gentry. But when Charles II became king, Blood's fortunes waned.

Blood blamed his downfall on James Butler, first duke of Ormandie and King Charles' lord lieutenant for Ireland. He plotted to kidnap the duke. The plan failed and Blood fled, a price on his head. His accomplices were executed.

In 1671, at 53, Blood—steeped in bitterness—blueprinted the atrocious foray to the tower and its treasure. The dazzling symbols of the monarchy were then kept in a niche behind an iron gate in Martin's Tower, in the northeast corner of the inner wall of the Tower of London.

Sir Gilbert Talbot was Keeper of the Regalia, and under law, he had to live where the king did. So, he turned the guarding of the crown jewels over to a poor, elderly kinsman, Talbot Edwards.

Edwards received nothing for his post of assistant keeper, but Charles II allowed him to show the jewels to anyone he thought trustworthy and to pocket any gratuities collected.

So, when a parson and his wife appeared April 21 of that year to see the sceptered grandeur, Edwards shuffled down from his third-floor apartment in Martin's Tower to show the gems in their first-floor cases. The second floor was unoccupied.

Seeing in the clergyman a good tip, Edwards showed the St. Edward's Crown, the State Crown, The King's Scepter, the jeweled orb.

Little did Edwards know that the "parson" was Blood and his "wife" a street harlot picked up for the occasion. As they left, the "wife" became faint and was helped to Edwards' apartment, where his wife gave her some spirits. The rogue left a generous gratuity.

A few days later, Edward's lady got four pairs of gloves from the "parson," and there were follow-up visits to the Tower. At one it was learned that Edwards had a marriageable daughter. Blood lied that he had a nephew making 300 pounds a year.

It was agreed that the two should meet at the tower May 9 at 7 a.m., a rather early hour. But years ago, men and maids were apparently different from today.

Blood arrived with the "nephew," Dick Halloway, a lookout; Blood's son-in-law, Thomas Hunt; and accomplice Robert Parrott, all armed. Blood suggested that Edwards show his guests the royal regalia until his "wife" arrived. Edwards let them into the viewing chamber and relocked the door behind him, as prescribed. Immediately, they fell upon the old man, gagged him and tethered him with a waxed leash.

"Be quiet, else harm will come to you," they warned.

But Edwards thrashed about until he was knocked out with a wooden mallet. With the keys from Edwards' pocket, they opened the grate and seized the jewels.

Blood found the St. Edward's Crown too heavy to carry off. He seized the State Crown and with the mallet flattened the crown's arches, knocking off its great ruby. The hammered crown now fit inside a sack Blood had brought.

Hunt stuck the jeweled orb inside his pants, while Parrott sawed the scepter in two so he could conceal it in his clothing.

At this crucial point, lookout Halloway banged on the door, shouting, "Trouble!"

Edwards' son Talbot, who had been fighting the Spanish in Flanders, had come home on a visit. Thinking Halloway a visitor, Talbot said he would call his father. But when he discovered at his apartment that the father was downstairs, Talbot became suspicious. He raced down to the jewel chamber.

But Blood and crew, alerted, had walked calmly away with the treasure. Talbot, finding the jewel case open and half looted, shouted, "Treason, Treason!"

He freed his father while members of the guard chased the thieves.

Meanwhile, the plunderers had walked unchallenged the length of the courtyard, under the Bloody Tower and along Water Lane to Bywater Tower. At this point the Yeoman of the Guard challenged them and was cut down by Blood's pistol.

"Stop, thief!" came the cry. Blood and his trio joined the chorus and pointed to other individuals who were seized. The thieves were at the Bulwark Gate, a few yards from safety, when a shattering realization struck Blood—he was at the West Gate. His getaway horses were at the Eastern Iron Gate.

Instantly, the four reversed course. Now Capt. John Beckenham of the London Tower guard, who was married to Edwards' other daughter, was upon them.

"Stop, thief, stop!" Blood brazenly cried, pointing to the out-of-uniform Beckenham. The crowd fell upon Beckenham, which gained precious minutes for the gem thieves. They had reached

Katherine's Tower and their horses by the time the crowd got to them, led by the now-exonerated Beckenham.

As the captain tried to grab Blood, the thief fired. Beckenham ducked and snatched from Blood's waist the sack containing the crown of England's monarch. It broke, shattering gold and gems over the road. Some jewels were never recovered.

Blood swung to his horse, but the animal slipped and the crowd grabbed the culprit. Parrott was yanked from his horse, and Halloway was seized before he could mount. Hunt galloped off, struck his head on a pole, was unseated and captured. By noon the battered jewels were back in the tower. Blood, jailed with his aides, insisted on seeing the king. Astonishingly, Charles II agreed. He liked bold men. He had never met one bolder than Blood.

They talked privately. Yet it was reported that Blood cautioned the 41-year-old monarch that Blood's followers could shake Charles loose from the throne. Switching to flattery, Blood purportedly told the vain ruler he had waited at Battersea to kill him while swimming, but his majesty's manly form, stripped for bathing, was of such grace and beauty, Blood tossed away his gun in awe.

Whatever worked, Blood and his partners were pardoned, his Irish estates were restored and he became a colonel in the king's own guard.

For nine years Blood labored fat and happy in the king's vineyard. But turbulence was a paramour Blood had too long courted to remain oblivious to its charms. He fell out with his friend, the Duke of Buckingham, and was jailed for slandering that noble presence.

Bailed while awaiting trial, Blood repaired to his Westminster home, where, on Aug. 24, 1680, he died—of natural causes—which surprised most who knew him.

Real-Life "On the Waterfront"

PATRICE O'SHAUGHNESSY

JULY 17, 1983

With only a few changes in names and details, the Academy Award–winning movie *On the Waterfront* could have told a true story about a real Brooklyn hero. But unlike the film that starred actor Marlon Brando, the real-life script for Peter Panto had no happy Hollywood ending.

Panto was a champion of the waterfront rank and file in the late 1930s, hated by the thugs who controlled the Brooklyn waterfront and revered by the longshoremen who suffered under them.

This was during the Depression, when Albert Anastasia and his fellow racketeers controlled the waterfront union, the International Longshoremen's Association (ILA) and enforced their rule through fear and violence; when the notorious shape-up—the system for hiring dock workers—would attract as many as 700 men competing for some 200 jobs. The jobs, by mob orders, went only to men willing to kick back part of their wages or perform other useful tasks—like ratting on any worker bold enough to complain about the situation.

There was also a "fugitive fund" for Murder Inc. hit men on the lam—every longshoreman was forced to contribute to it.

Eventually, it all made Panto as mad as hell and he decided he wouldn't take it anymore.

At 28, he was dark-haired and mustachioed, with sharp features and an imposing manner—the type to command attention, if not respect—and he began his crusade by inspiring supporters, mainly Italian immigrants, with speeches at meetings held near the Brooklyn waterfront area.

Panto's message was simple: Dock workers should form an independent union, even if it was sure to draw violent resistance from the gangster-ruled ILA.

As attendance at the meetings grew, the mob offered him cushy, no-show jobs. Panto said no. Next, it spread the always-effective propaganda of the day—it labeled Panto a Communist. He ignored it; so did his followers. Panto continued his flamboyant, outspoken crusade.

He had been a stevedore for about 10 years, when, in 1939, he brazenly denounced Anastasia—the boss of bosses and controller of the Brooklyn rackets—and his triggerman, Anthony "Tony Spring" Romeo, for forcing workers to kick back part of their pay in return for jobs.

Panto's fate was decided at a meeting held July 8, 1939, at Star Hall on Carroll St. Union elections were coming up, and Panto was pushing for the organization of forklift drivers. About 1,250 longshoremen cheered Panto's campaign—and two of Anastasia's spies took it all in.

When they reported the goings-on to their boss, he realized that the rebel Panto had become a serious threat to the mob's survival on the docks. A contract was put out on the insurgent unionist's life.

A week later, on July 14, according to author and mob historian Will Balsamo, two men showed up at the door to Panto's rented Brooklyn house while Panto was getting ready to take his girlfriend to the beach. The two ordered Panto into their car. Panto told his girl that he was going to meet a "couple of tough guys" and that he would return in an hour or so. Then he left.

With that, Panto dropped out of sight—for good.

Months went by, but his rank-and-file followers did not forget. Fifteen months later, in October of 1940, the new leader of the reform movement, Peter Mazzie, who was only 23, pledged to carry on Panto's program and to fulfill his plan to break away form corrupt union leaders and form an independent local. The meetings continued, even though they often ended up as riots incited by strong-arm ILA henchmen.

Meanwhile, a Pete Panto memorial committee was formed. Its members asked the Brooklyn district attorney, William O'Dwyer, to find and punish Panto's killers. O'Dwyer dismissed Panto as a Communist and put the case on the back burner.

All over the waterfront, Panto's pals scrawled reminders on the walls and sidewalks. "Where is Peter Panto?" one read. "Who killed Peter Panto?" read another. Nobody came forward to answer either question.

In January 1941, Abe "Kid Twist" Reles, a notorious mobster under indictment for murder, decided to turn on his pals to save himself. Among other things, he told O'Dwyer that what he knew could clear up several unsolved Brooklyn murders. One of the victims, Reles said, was Peter Panto.

Reles, a squat, cold-blooded thug who bragged that he had personally killed 11 men, told O'Dwyer that the two men who picked up Panto at his home that July night in 1939 took him to see Romeo and three members of the murder syndicate, Jimmy "Dirty Face" Feraco, Jimmy Florino and Emanuel "Mendy" Weiss, who spoke on Anastasia's behalf.

At the meeting, Reles said, Weiss, a 6-foot, 200-pound brawler, offered Panto $10,000 to keep his mouth shut and stop the union organizing. But Panto said no—his last act of defiance.

Weiss strangled Panto on the spot, according to Reles. The body was dumped in an isolated area on the banks of the Passaic River in Lyndhurst, N.J., a favorite mob disposal area.

Acting on Reles' story, New Jersey cops searched the site on Jan. 29 and found the remains of two men encased in quicklime. Mazzie identified one of the bodies as that of Peter Panto.

On the basis of Reles' testimony, O'Dwyer charged Weiss with the murder. At the time, Weiss was a fugitive—on the run for nearly two years because he was wanted in the murder of one Joseph Rosen, a Brooklyn candy store owner gunned down before he could testify in a rackets investigation.

The cops finally caught up with Weiss in Kansas City on April 5, 1941. He never went on trial for killing Panto, but he did stand trial in the Rosen case. He was convicted and died in the electric chair in 1944.

Feraco and Florino disappeared. The gossip was that they were rubbed out by their pals because Murder Inc. was afraid that Reles' talkative habit was catching.

As for Reles, he fell, jumped or was pushed from an upper-floor room of the Half Moon Hotel in Coney Island, where police were guarding him during questioning. The more cynical sort insisted Reles was pushed. To this day, it remains one of the city's most sensational unsolved cases.

Romeo did not die a natural death, either. His bullet-riddled body was found on a wooded knoll near Wilmington, Del.

Officially, Panto's murder remains unsolved.

His memory was harder to kill. As late as the 1940s and '50s, union reformers and rebels on the waterfront would hear the old warning, "You'll wind up like Pete Panto."

In 1981, Balsamo recalled, when the ILA and its officials were investigated by the FBI for extortion and bribery schemes on piers from New York to Miami, someone passed around a newsletter calling for reform on the waterfront. In it was a photo of Peter Panto.

The "Crime"-50 Years Later

JOSEPH MCNAMARA
FEBRUARY 10, 1985

O n the cold night of Feb. 13, 1935, a jury of four women and eight men in bucolic Flemington, N.J., announced to a breathless world that they had found Bruno Richard Hauptmann guilty of the kidnap-murder of Charles A. Lindbergh Jr.

A mighty cheer went up from crowds outside the tiny Hunterdon County courthouse on Main St., throngs that patiently had waited the entire one hour and 24 minutes the panel pondered.

The guilty verdict climaxed what has often been called the Trial of the Century, a six-week flood of millions of words that the irreverent H.L. Mencken dubbed "the greatest story since the Resurrection." More than 300 reporters and photographers, countless celebrities, lawyers and the curious vied for courtroom space, prompting Sheriff John Curtis to moan, "The trial should have been held in Madison Square Garden."

Some vendors thought it was. They hawked Lindbergh baby dolls and tiny wood versions of the kidnap ladder, and much seemed like carnival. Still, mighty matters were at stake. Hauptmann, 36, a German-born carpenter, was fighting for survival against a prosecution case of circumstantial evidence so classic that it has been used as a text at Harvard Law School.

But public sympathy was plainly with the family of the victim, a 20-month-old blond boy with blue eyes whose body, its skull fractured, had been found May 12, 1932, alongside a road five miles from the Lindbergh home outside Hopewell.

Lindbergh—Lucky Lindy, the Lone Eagle, idolized as few men in history following his stirring 1927 transatlantic flight to Paris—and his wife, Anne Morrow, rode high in public favor in this, their moment of grief.

It all began the raw and windy night of March 1, 1932, at the Lindberghs' not-yet-finished twin-gabled white mansion high on Sourland Mountain. At 9:15 Lindbergh, chatting with Anne in the ground-floor library, heard a noise like an "orange crate slat falling off a chair." He thought it came from the kitchen, where domestics Oliver and Elsie Whately were. At 10 the baby's nurse, Betty Gow, noticed that his crib in the upstairs nursery was empty.

The Lindberghs rushed to the nursery, found mud trailed from the crib to a window and a ransom note on the windowsill. It demanded $50,000 for return of the child. It was signed with a three-circle symbol.

"Anne," cried Lindbergh, "they have stolen our baby!"

Police were summoned. They found behind a clump of bushes near the house a handmade ladder with one rung broken, obviously used by the kidnaper to reach the second-floor window. And 100 feet away was the baby's discarded bedding.

Investigators at first suspected an inside job. How did anyone know the baby would be there that Tuesday night? Normally, the Lindberghs would have returned with him Sunday night to Anne's mother's home in Englewood, where they had been living pending completion of their own home on 500 secluded acres. They had stayed at Hopewell just on weekends. However, little Charles had a cold that weekend, and Anne decided to stay over.

State police questioned the Whatelys and Betty Gow at length, then turned to Violet Sharpe, a maid in the home of Anne's mother, Mrs. Dwight Morrow. Violet had been stepping out on her steady beau and gave cops evasive answers. This led to further, relentless questioning, with Violet subsequently killing herself with poison. Later she was exonerated of any blame in the kidnaping.

The crime stirred international outrage and fury. Everybody played detective. *The Bronx Home News* asked an educator, John Condon, 74, what he thought. Condon offered in print to give $1,000 reward money and act as intermediary with the kidnapers. This was seven days after the kidnaping. The next day Condon was astonished to be taken at his word. A note from the kidnaper was delivered by a Bronx cabbie.

Condon met the kidnaper in Bronx's Woodlawn Cemetery and in Cortlandt Park and arranged payment of the $50,000 ransom after receiving 13 notes. Like the note found in the baby's nursery, these were signed with the three-circle symbol, were poorly spelled and in German script. On March 16, the sleeping suit the baby had worn was delivered to Condon's home.

On April 2, a box fashioned by the U.S. Treasury and containing the $50,000 ransom was tossed over a hedge in St. Raymond's Cemetery to a man who cried, "Hey, Doktor!" Lindbergh, 100 yards away, heard the words. For his money, Lindy got a note informing him his son was on a boat, the *Nellie,* off Gay Head, Mass. No such vessel was found.

On May 12, the baby's body was found in a shallow grave, badly decomposed, dead an estimated 10 weeks. It was believed the child suffered his fatal head injury when he struck the house wall as the ladder rung broke under the kidnaper. This was apparently the noise Lindbergh had heard.

Condon told authorities the man he had met was a German or Scandinavian with broad forehead, square jaw and piercing eyes. He scanned thousands of mug shots but came up dry. For a brief time he came under suspicion himself.

Meanwhile, the ransom money began to show up in the Bronx and Manhattan, $2,980 by May 1, 1933. On that date the Treasury called back its gold certificates, as the U.S. went off the gold standard. Much of the ransom had been paid in gold notes, which now became scarce.

Sixteen months later, a $10 gold note was given to a gas station attendant at 127th St. and Lexington Ave. He jotted on the bill the license number of the auto. The plate was traced to Hauptmann.

In Hauptmann's Bronx garage, cops found $14,600 more ransom money in the distinctive Treasury box. Hauptmann claimed it had been given to him by a friend, Isador Fisch, who had gone back to Germany to die of TB. Investigators, though, established that Fisch had been penniless, had slept some nights in Grand Central terminal.

Wood in the ladder was traced to the attic of Hauptmann's home. Probers claimed nail holes in the wood matched holes in beams in the house. On Sept. 19, 1934, Hauptmann was arrested. And the following January, he went on trial.

The witnesses were persuasive. Bronx cabbie Joseph Perrone swore Hauptmann gave him $1 on March 12, 1932, to deliver a letter to Condon's home. Amandus Hochmuth, 87, testified he saw Hauptmann drive past his Hopewell home with a ladder in his car, heading toward the Lindbergh estate the day of the kidnaping. Federal wood expert Arthur Koehler swore he traced the wood in the ladder from a South Carolina mill to a Bronx lumberyard where Hauptmann once worked. He identified one piece of the ladder as coming from the defendant's attic.

Lindbergh himself testified it was Hauptmann's "Hey, Doktor" he had heard in the cemetery.

New Jersey attorney general David T. Wilentz, 39, prosecuted the case. He hammered away at Hauptmann on the stand, a blistering assault that hard-drinking defense counsel Edward Reilly did little to blunt. Hauptmann insisted he was innocent, but the jury believed otherwise.

After a number of delays, Hauptmann went to the electric chair in Trenton State Prison on April 3, 1936. In March 1977, a 5,000-word letter which Hauptmann had written his mother in Germany surfaced. The letter, penned Dec. 27, 1935, had been impounded by prison officials. In it, Hauptmann swore his innocence and accused his defense counsel of "working with the prosecutor."

Some still believe Hauptmann was the victim of mass hysteria. His widow, Anna, 86, charged that the State of New Jersey murdered her innocent husband. She filed a federal lawsuit asking $100 million in damages on grounds Wilentz "knowingly presented perjured testimony" and withheld "exculpatory evidence." She also named other officials. Wilentz, at 89 still practicing law, denies all the allegations, calling them nonsense.

On April 5, 1984, federal judge Fred A. Lacey in Newark threw out the complaint on the grounds that the statute of limitations had expired on most allegations and that others failed to support her suit. Anna filed a second wrongful-death lawsuit two years later that was also dismissed by the federal court.

Anna Hauptmann's Fight Ends

JAY MAEDER
OCTOBER 19, 1994

I n the end, Jersey Justice wore Anna Hauptmann down.

She quietly passed away last week at 95, having finally and forlornly abandoned her epic crusade to clear the name of the long-dead husband many historians believe wrongly paid for one of the nation's most enduringly sensational crimes

One of the last remaining links to the 1932 kidnap-slaying of aviator Charles Lindbergh's baby son, Mrs. Hauptmann died in New Holland, Pa., Oct. 10—the 69th anniversary of her marriage to Bruno Richard Hauptmann of the Bronx.

"They wanted her to die and go away," snapped San Francisco lawyer Robert Bryan, who had represented Anna Hauptmann through years of futile federal litigation in what he insists remains 60 years later a politically sensitive case in New Jersey. "They got their wish."

Once certain that an avalanche of newly emerged evidence would overturn history's judgment of her husband's role in the Lindbergh affair, the old woman "had become discouraged," Bryan told the *Daily News* last night. "She talked constantly about death. She said, 'I should have died 10 years ago and been with Richard.'"

Bryan's labyrinthine civil suit collapsed several years ago with rulings that the public officials who allegedly railroaded Hauptmann with manufactured evidence and perjured trial witnesses were immune from prosecution. More recently, he had petitioned New Jersey legislators—and two governors—for posthumous executive clemency.

Former Gov. Jim Florio "wouldn't talk to us," he said. "He wouldn't give us 10 minutes. We were hopeful when Gov. [Christine Todd] Whitman came in that she would be more sensitive to Mrs. Hauptmann. But I wrote her last February, and she hasn't responded yet."

Richard Hauptmann—he was called Bruno only by prosecutors and the press—was convicted of the Lindbergh kidnaping chiefly because $14,000 of the ransom cash was found in his Bronx garage. The nation jeered at the stammered explanation that a friend had left it with him for safekeeping, but in recent years, many books and articles reexamining the famous old case have concluded he was telling the truth.

And thousands of FBI and New Jersey state police documents unearthed by Bryan in the 1980s appear to support revisionist contentions that much of the damning testimony against Hauptmann— including Lindbergh's own—was patently false.

Hauptmann died in the electric chair in Trenton in April 1936, swearing his innocence. Among those who believed him was then-Gov. Harold Hoffman, who stayed the execution several times and later wrote a series of articles alleging police and prosecutorial corruption.

Bryan said he will continue to fight for Hauptmann's exoneration. "I owe it to Mrs. Hauptmann," he said.

In an interview published in the *Daily News Magazine* in 1988. Anna Hauptmann reflected on the powerful officials who made the case against her husband:

"The pity I feel for the people who do this thing. Ach, they stoop so low. How must they feel thinking, ach, I was the one who sent that man to his death. Because they know. They know. They all have to die, and with all their money and with all their titles they will go the same way, and when their hour comes they will be afraid.

"I am not afraid."

Undying Dillinger Legend

Joseph McNamara

July 15, 1984

Half a century has passed since that torrid July night when John Herbert Dillinger, betrayed by the Woman in Red, was shot down by federal agents outside the Biograph Theater on Chicago's north side.

To some people a folk hero, to all an accomplished bank robber and killer, Dillinger was labeled Public Enemy No. 1 and the "Arch Criminal of the Century." Reckless daring and disdain for authority, coupled with massive doses of publicity, gave Dillinger an aura of invincibility in a nation racked by the Great Depression.

After all, in the previous 10 months the Dillinger mob had robbed some 20 midwestern banks of $300,000, killed 10 men and wounded seven, looted three police arsenals of arms and bulletproof vests and staged three sensational prison breaks. The Indiana National Guard had wanted to use tanks, airplanes and poison gas on the desperado. And the American Legion had offered to arm 30,000 members as vigilantes to aid in his capture.

On that fateful night of July 22, 1934, it took only a handful of agents, three firing their pistols, to claim the life of the most infamous criminal in America. He had just turned 31.

Dillinger was born June 22, 1903, in the Oak Hill Subdivision of Indianapolis to an immigrant father, John W., and Millie (Landcaster), who died when he was three. An older sister raised him. The father, a grocer, owned four rental houses, and money did not seem to be a problem But the boy, not fond of work, fretted under the old man's domination.

In 1913 the Pennsylvania Railroad cracked down on the "Dirty Dozen Gang," kids who had stolen tons of coal from railroad gondolas and were selling cheap to homeowners. Nailed by railroad detectives, the youthful criminals were hauled before a judge, all but one repentant. This lad, the leader, chewed gum and wore his cap cocked over one eye.

"Your mind is crippled," the judge told Dillinger, then 10.

At 16 Dillinger quit school. His father bought a 60-acre farm in Mooresville, Ind., but the slight youth—5-foot-7, 160 pounds— did most of his "farming" in the town's pool room. He joined the navy and was berthed on the battleship *Utah*. When it made Boston harbor Dec. 4, 1923, Dillinger deserted. The following April 12, he married a pretty farm girl, Berl Hovious, but they were divorced in June 1929 while John was in prison.

This stretch was imposed for Dillinger's first major crime, the attempted robbery of a Mooresville grocer. John and an ex-con underestimated the strength of the victim, 65, who tussled with them, and Dillinger's .32 pistol went off. Dillinger drew two to 14 years and 10 to 20 on charges of assault and battery with intent to rob and conspiracy to commit a felony. His confederate, before a different judge, got a far lighter sentence. This embittered Dillinger.

In May 1933, after eight years in stir, Dillinger was paroled from Michigan City Penitentiary and came back to a different world than the prosperous one he had left. Millions of jobless men roamed the streets, hundreds of banks had folded, wiping out the savings of the populace, and thousands of businesses were bankrupt.

During the Prohibition era then ending, big-time gangsters came into their own. Pretty Boy Floyd, Bonnie and Clyde, Machine Gun Kelly and the Barker-Karpis gang, among others, robbed banks over wide areas, and there were virtually no federal laws to impede them.

To many who lost money to defaulting bankers, machine-gun banditry was merely an alternate form of employment. One reader wrote to an Indianapolis newspaper about Dillinger: "He robbed those who became rich by robbing the poor, I am for Johnny."

Dillinger now turned to the trade he had learned in prison—robbing banks. At the Indiana reformatory at Pendleton and later at the Michigan City pen, Dillinger met master bandits such as Harry Pierpont, John Hamilton and Homer Van Meter, and once out, he determined to free them. For this he needed money. Many of his first heists netted puny sums. But then he pulled a $10,000 bank robbery and a payroll stickup worth $24,000, goodly amounts for that day. Palms were greased and a Chicago thread maker was bribed to conceal several guns inside a barrel shipped to the prison's shirt shop. The barrel was marked with a red X, so the prisoners would recognize it.

On Sept. 26, 1933, Pierpont and nine others took several hostages and made their escape from Michigan City. In the meantime, Dillinger himself, recognized during his crime binge, had been arrested in Dayton, Ohio, while visiting a new girlfriend. Pierpont returned Dillinger's favor, breaking him out of jail in Lima, Ohio, and fatally wounding Sheriff Jess Sarber in the process.

After a string of bank heists, the mob vacationed in Florida and then in Tucson, Ariz., where Dillinger, his moll Billie Frechette,

Pierpont and several others were arrested. Dillinger was flown back to Chicago, and the 40-officer "Dillinger Squad" and 85 other cops met the plane. A 13-car convoy brought him to the "escape-proof" jail in Crown Heights, Ind.

The first thing Dillinger did, of course, was to escape, on March 3, 1934. He took another prisoner and two hostages, whom he gallantly gave $4 for carfare when he released them.

With his lieutenants imprisoned, Dillinger put together another mob, which included a wild punk named Lester Gillis "Baby Face" Nelson. A quick string of robberies provided defense money for Pierpont and the others in jail. But it did little good. Pierpont was later electrocuted for the murder of Sheriff Sarber.

Now, the feds were on Dillinger's tail, a result of a stolen car crossing the Illinois state line. His greater crimes were local matters. In St. Paul, Dillinger was wounded in the leg by agents of the Justice Department's Division of Investigation, which later became the FBI. In April, at the Little Bohemia Lodge 50 miles outside Rhinelander, Wis., the gang slipped away while agents killed an innocent patron and wounded two others. Nelson shot to death a special agent and wounded a cop.

But the clock was running down on Dillinger. He underwent plastic surgery on his face and had his fingerprints altered to frustrate pursuing lawmen. And then it was July, and the Lady in Red, Anna Sage (real name Ana Cumpanas), saw a chance to escape deportation to her native Romania and also pick up the $15,000 reward money on Dillinger's head.

Sage, 42, was being deported as an undesirable alien because she had run a bawdy house in Gary, Ind. Sage's girlfriend, Polly Hamilton, had taken up with a new beau, a Jimmy Lawrence, whom Anna recognized as Dillinger. Through a contact with East Chicago police, Sage made a deal with the feds to betray Dillinger. Melvin Purvis, federal agent in charge of Chicago, said he would do what he could with immigration authorities.

On July 22 Sage informed Purvis that Lawrence was taking Polly and her to the movies that night. She wasn't sure whether it would be the Biograph or the Marlboro film house—Lawrence would not commit himself. Both theaters were staked out by federal and local officers.

Dillinger showed up at the Biograph in 101-degree heat, wearing a white silk shirt, gray pants and dark glasses. He sported a new mustache. He had Polly on one arm, Anna—wearing a red dress, as prearranged, so she would be recognized—on the other. Purvis had planned to move into a seat behind Dillinger and seize him from behind. But once Dillinger was seated, agents found the nearest empty seat three rows away. Purvis decided to make the collar after the movie, *Manhattan Melodrama,* in which "gangster" Clark Gable went to the electric chair.

As the trio left the theater, Purvis, standing in a doorway, lit his cigar, a signal that he had recognized Dillinger. Anna and Hamilton fell back and agents approached the gangster.

"All right, Johnny . . . " one began.

Dillinger whirled, realized he was trapped, raced for an alley and reached for a pistol in his pants pocket. Shots rang out. One caught Dillinger in the side. A fatal one, as he fell, hit him in the back and emerged from his right eye. He was dead when he hit the pavement. There was $7.80 in his pocket.

Purvis, ripping the buttons from his jacket to get out his pistol, fired the shots with two other agents. They never revealed whose bullets brought down gangdom's superstar.

Hysteria followed. Thousands showed up to view the body. Many refused to accept the victim as Dillinger, their suspicions partly abetted by a bungled autopsy, which reported Dillinger's eyes as brown. His military records listed them as blue.

As recently as the previous March, Cook County medical examiner Robert E. Stein, who worked on the autopsy, declared that a missing report had been found, and it confirmed that the slain man was Dillinger. The report, lost years ago, showed up in a shopping bag in the ME's office during a move to new quarters. Stein downplayed the eye coloration.

"After death, there can be some clouding of the cornea and you could have difficulty telling the color of the iris," he declared.

"There's no question in my mind the man killed at the Biograph was Dillinger."

The Lady in Red? She got $5,000 of the reward money. But she was deported to Romania, where she died in 1947.

The Long Search for Typhoid Mary

JOSEPH MCNAMARA
NOVEMBER 3, 1985

Fear of a deadly disease is as native to mankind as anguish over the unknown—and often one feeds the other—whether it be leprosy in biblical times or AIDS in our own. As the 20th century dawned on New Yorkers, typhoid was the insidious illness. And the pariah of that era, and perhaps of this era, was the "carrier"—the person who, showing no signs of the malady, harbors the germs that infect others.

Most infamous of the local carriers, possibly because she was the first so recognized, was Mary Mallon, 40ish and jovial, a neat, plump, good-looking cook of Irish extraction. She was great with the skillet and easily found work in the better homes and institutions of the day. But when she left, as she did hastily, the inmates battled fevers as high as 105 degrees and intestinal distress that sometimes led to death. Mary was a living fount of the bacillus typhus.

In time she became known and shunned as Typhoid Mary. And unmasking her was a clever piece of detective work.

Mary's tragic story began in 1900, when a mysterious typhoid outbreak erupted in Mamaroneck—mysterious because the food and water supply there appeared above reproach. The typhoid germ enters the body through infected food or drink.

In 1902 seven persons came down with fever in the home of J. Coleman Drayton in Dark Harbor, Maine. And in 1904 typhoid hit the residence of Henry Gilsey in Sands Point, L.I., and homes in Oyster Bay and Tuxedo Park. There was one death. Puzzled because the water and food seemed safe, the New York Health Department called in Dr. George A. Soper, a renowned sanitary engineer consultant and avid investigator.

Although the typhoid germ was isolated in 1884, it was many years before Dr. Robert Koch, a noted German bacteriologist, discovered that the disease could be spread by an apparently healthy person. Dr. Koch traced repeated outbreaks in Strassburg to a bakery where the woman proprietor had suffered typhoid years before. He tested her and found that, although no longer ill, she still gave off typhoid germs. The carrier principle had been discovered.

News of Koch's find reached America in 1904, and Soper greeted it with interest. He studied these homes that had been visited by typhoid and learned that Mary Mallon had been a cook in each when the disease struck.

But the fair-haired Mary was not to be found. Unlettered in medicine, she instinctively fled each time the fever raged around her. Soper and his men worked through employment agencies, and in March 1907 they found Mary working in a Park Avenue house, where she was highly regarded by both the owners and other servants.

Dr. S. Josephine Baker, head of the Health Department's Child Hygiene Bureau, was assigned to examine Mary Mallon. But Mary refused to permit it. The next day Dr. Baker returned to the house with three policemen and an ambulance full of interns. They searched the premises for two hours before finding Mary hiding behind two garbage cans under a rear porch.

The terrified woman screamed, kicked and bit, but she was overcome and put in the ambulance. Dr. Baker sat on her chest all the way to Willard Parker Hospital, where tests confirmed that Mary was indeed a repository of typhoid germs. She was quarantined on North Brother Island in the East River.

Officials urged Mary to undergo surgery for removal of her gallbladder, the usual hatchery for such germs. She viewed this as a Health Department "attempt to murder me."

In 1909 she angrily sought a State Supreme Court order for her freedom. She charged she had been locked up like a leper for two years with only a dog for company, that her food was shoved through her grilled door by a nurse who fled in terror. Her attorney, George O'Neill, asked if a person who has committed no crime can be locked up indefinitely because someone says she has germs. The judge noted that, under the city charter, the Health Department has broad powers to isolate persons considered dangerous to the public health. And he refused her bid.

"Before God and the eyes of decent men I was christened Mary Mallon and lived a decent, upright life until I was seized by the city, locked up in a pest house and rechristened Typhoid Mary," she wailed in an interview in the *New York World.*

The Health Department relented. On Feb. 10, 1910, it released Mary Mallon, convinced she now realized how dangerous she was and sure she would live up to her promise never to handle food. Mary's hands were lethal. Under her fingernails lurked an unseen but real peril.

Mary "kept straight" for a while. Then in 1914, typhoid flared in a sanitarium in Newfoundland, N.J. It was discovered that Mary had been a cook there and was now gone. Apparently, cooking was the only way she could earn a living. In Sloan Maternity Hospital, Manhattan, 25 person got the fever, and two died. On the cooking staff was a "Mrs. Brown." She was really Typhoid Mary.

Mary was watched by police and health officials. That afternoon, she left the hospital with a bowl of gelatin for friends in Corona, Queens. As she approached the house, she was heavily veiled. The affable Mary Mallon had become sly, devious, suspicious. She was seized inside the house.

Bitter and sullen, Mary Mallon was returned to North Brother Island, which would be her home for the last 24 years of her life. For nine years she was morose, moody, quizzical of a fate she could not understand, railing at a punishment she felt she did not deserve.

A sympathetic staff never gave up on her and eventually re-established her faith in herself. She got a job in the hospital laboratories at $60 a month, and this enabled her to buy the books she wanted. She loved Charles Dickens.

Her Roman Catholicism was solace to her in later years, friends said. And she did make friends, with doctors, nurses and attendants. In 1923 the City of New York did something to make Mary's years more livable—it built her a house on the island. In her 20-by-20-foot one-story, green-shingled cottage with an elm tree on the front lawn, Mary Mallon entertained her friends. But they never stayed for supper. A good cook to the end, Mary prepared the meals and ate alone. She had a tan mutt for company. Mary Mallon carried the official designation "Carrier No. 36." Though the first discovered, she and many others were categorized at one time alphabetically. Her listed toll was 51 original cases of typhoid, three deaths. But officials feel the actual toll was much higher.

She was not the most deadly, though. In 1909 in Manhattan and the Bronx, 409 cases of typhoid and 40 deaths were traced to a dairy farmer in Camden, N.Y., who had had the disease 46 years before. Mary claimed she had never had typhoid, but some felt she might have had a mild case and did not recognize it as such.

On Christmas Day 1932, Mary suffered a paralytic stroke and lingered in an isolation ward in Riverside Hospital on the island until her death on Nov. 11, 1938. Her listed age was 70. Mary's past died with her. All that is known is that she said she was born in the United States, but refused to say where. She had never married.

Typhoid is no longer the scourge it once was, thanks to inoculation, modern medicines and monitoring techniques the Board of Health conducts as a result of the experience with Typhoid Mary. Last year there were 26 cases of typhoid in the city, down from 46 the year before, according to Assistant Health Commissioner Marvin Bogner.

Bogner noted there are 300 registered carriers in the city, who are checked annually and strictly enjoined from handling food or caring for the sick.

"Typhoid is not a problem here today," Bogner said.

Today's problem is destruction of the body's immune system. It has created a dread as great as any stirred by Typhoid Mary. It has even prompted a State Supreme Court justice to ask if AIDS victims should not be quarantined, as Mary Mallon was for 27 years.

The Bloody White Hands

CHARLES W. BELL
AUGUST 15, 1982

T he White Hand gang that ruled the Brooklyn docks for about 20 years, starting around 1910, elected bosses in a highly novel way—by tossing a pair of unloaded dice. The first candidate who rolled a seven was boss.

However, good luck wasn't everything.

For example, on May 16, 1928, Eddie McGuire, whose nickname was "Lucky," rolled the first seven. He was boss for all of five minutes before he was shot and killed. The police blamed one of the unsuccessful candidates, Charles "Cute Charlie" Donnelly, and three of his supporters.

The case against the four was dismissed by Judge Leo Healy, who told Donnelly and Co. as they walked out of the courtroom,

"Go out and keep up the good work. Kill one another off just as fast as you can."

About 18 months later, Donnelly was sitting in his office, in a dockland shack, when someone ended his term of office with a volley of shots.

So it went with the Irish toughs of the White Hand, a name that crime historians contend was chosen to mock the Black Hand, an equally vicious and ambitious gang of Italian toughs who specialized in bootlegging, gambling and—of all things—rolling drunks.

There were other gangs of the era, but on the Brooklyn docks, the rivals were the White Hands, who specialized in hijacking, extortion and kickbacks, and the Black Hands, who were starting to realize the big money was in bootlegging and drugs. The two gangs were bitter enemies, and it was this mutual hatred—and the profits of crime—that led to a sensational Roaring Twenties murder case. One with a special twist.

It happened on Dec. 26, 1925, in a dive called the Adonis Social and Athletic Club on 20th St., in a South Brooklyn area controlled by Italian gangsters and run by one John Stabile, who called himself Jack Stickum—after his favorite English-language phrase, which was "Stick 'em up!"

There were three victims, but the one who made headlines was Richard "Peg Leg" Lonergan, a notorious braggart, bully and boozer who took over the gang from his brother-in-law, Wild Bill Lovett.

After his marriage to Peg Leg's sister, Anna, the much-feared Lovett retired from the day-to-day supervision of White Hand activities and moved to Little Ferry, N.J. Still, he could not resist an occasional visit to the gang's Brooklyn hangout. It was there that

Lovett was found shot to death on Halloween 1931. (Because he had won a Distinguished Service Cross on the battlefields of France during World War I, he was buried with full military honors.)

Lonergan then took over, to the surprise of some observers who wondered if a man missing his right leg—severed in a railroad accident when he was 21—could impose his will. However, his skills with fists, clubs, knives and guns persuaded his rivals that he had the right leadership stuff.

In any case, the White Hands continued to exact tribute from barge and wharf owners. Those who refused were beaten, stabbed or shot and their property looted, wrecked or burned. But the White Hands coveted the South Brooklyn turf that the Italians controlled.

By Christmas 1925, the feud was going full blast.

Despite its name, the Adonis Social and Athletic Club was not a health spa or sports hangout but a dingy speakeasy run by and for Italians, with a tiny back room illuminated by orange light bulbs and used for dancing and dining.

An all-day Christmas party was just breaking up when Lonergan and five of his henchmen appeared at the club just after midnight, demanding drinks and shouting ethnic slurs.

According to survivors, several people inside the club sat quietly for a few minutes as the Lonergan gang grew noisier and more abusive. Suddenly, one of the "customers" pulled a meat cleaver from his coat and split the skull of Aaron Harms, a Lonergan lieutenant. Within seconds, gunfire erupted.

About five minutes later, a cop named Richard Morano spotted a man in the gutter about half a block from the club. Thinking it was just another Christmas-party drunk, Morano went over to rouse the man. He couldn't—the man was dead, of severe head wounds. It was Harms, and a bloody trail led from his body to the open door of the Adonis.

Inside the club, slumped over a table, was the body of Cornelius "Needles" Ferry, a Lonergan aide. Sprawled behind a piano in one corner was the body of another man; and even in the dim light, Morano recognized him—it was Lonergan.

To investigators, it looked like an ambush. Lonergan's mother told police that Peg Leg had left home about 9 p.m., telling her that he was going to buy Christmas tree decorations. But he told his henchmen they were going to the Adonis, and it turned out that one of them, a turncoat named Eddie Lynch, had tipped off the Italian gang.

About an hour after the shooting, one James Hart turned up at an area hospital with bullet wounds in the leg and one ear. He said that he was shot from a passing car as he was taking a stroll. Club employees, however, said he was a Lonergan pal who had been in the Adonis with his boss.

As is usual in such cases, an amnesia epidemic broke out among witnesses. But gradually, police learned the names of the people in the club, or at least some of them. Stabile was present, along with his bartenders and bouncers, Anthony Desso, Ralph D'Amato, Frank Pizza, George Carozza and Sylvester Agoglia.

And, surprise! Al Capone.

And what was the Boss himself doing at the club?

It was no big deal, said Capone, who told police that he lived at 377 18th St., a few blocks from the Adonis. "I was visiting my mother for Christmas," he said "and as a favor, I was working as the doorman at the club."

He was much too modest. By 1925, "Scarface Al" Capone, a Brooklyn boy, had moved to Cicero, Ill., and had become a national crime figure, as the head of a bootlegging, gambling and prostitution empire.

Perhaps for this reason, authorities did not buy the "doorman" story, and so, on Dec. 31, Capone was arraigned in Magistrate's Court on homicide charges, along with D'Amato, Pizza, Carozza, Desso, Stabile, Agoglia, plus Lonergan loyalists Joe Howard, John Maloney and James Hart.

Magistrate Francis McCloskey dismissed the murder charges, but as soon as the defendants left the courtroom, they were nabbed again and charged with assault on Hart. However, when they appeared in Magistrate's Court again, lawyer Samuel Leibowitz produced an affidavit signed by Hart. The affidavit exonerated Capone and everyone else of any wrongdoing. The assault charges also were dismissed.

According to William Balsamo, a Brooklyn writer who has interviewed many old gangland figures and studied the official case files, Capone was indeed one of the triggermen, along with John Scalisi and Albert Anselmi, two other Chicago hoodlums who came East at the request of Brooklyn Compatriots who wanted Lonergan dead.

"It was the most important murder of Capone's career," Balsamo said. "It just about ended the influence of the White Hands, and Capone's reputation really zoomed because of the Adonis job."

Perhaps. In any case, it was the last time that Al Capone's name would appear on a homicide warrant.

The Killer Called Baby Face

JOSEPH MCNAMARA
NOVEMBER 25, 1984

For pure viciousness, exhilaration in the act of killing, no participant in the saga of American crime could match Lester M. Gillis. "Lester who?" you may ask. Try George Nelson. Or, better yet, Baby Face Nelson.

Nelson soaked up 17 slugs in a wild shootout with two federal agents that left all three fatally wounded in a Chicago suburb on Nov. 27, 1934. At that time the Justice Department said Nelson was the only man who had killed more than one of its operatives. He was blamed for three.

This swagging, bantam killer—5-feet-5, 133 pounds—liked to call himself Big George Nelson. No one called him Baby Face in his presence any more than prudent men called Charles Arthur Floyd Pretty Boy to his face. His wife called him Les. The feds called him Public Enemy No. 1 and put a $5,000 reward on his head. U.S. attorney general Homer S. Cummings simply called him Rat. When Nelson died at 25, half his life had been spent stealing cars, bootlegging, robbing banks, serving time, killing and bragging.

Lester Gillis was born in Chicago Dec. 6, 1908, of Belgian immigrant parents. His father, a tanner, died when Lester was a child, and he soon proved more than his mother, Mary, could handle. He grew up in the stockyard district, ruled by toughs called the Five Points Gang, where the name Lester brought a quick snicker followed by a quicker fight. The hot-tempered punk became proficient with the "poor boy's equalizer"—the switchblade knife. And in time he got respect, if not acceptance. He befriended another misfit—pimply, heart-troubled Francis Albin Karpoviecz, who later wrote his own adopted name into the crime annals—Alvin Karpis.

To show he was tough, Gillis began stealing cars. At 14 he was sent to a reform school. For the next four years he was in and out of custody. He refused to return to school, settling for the one he attended with other criminals, majoring in theft and bank robbery.

Blue-eyed and blond, he gave the appearance of boyishness, which constantly goaded him to violence. In one of his early busts, he gave police the name George Nelson, and lawmen chased him under this moniker to his dying day.

At 18, Nelson drifted west, stealing cars for transportation and robbing gas stations for expenses. In Reno he became chauffeur for a gambler and liked the flow of money. But he was no gambler. Nelson moved on to Los Angeles and bootlegging. He did quite well there, but San Francisco beckoned—a wide-open town where no one paid any attention to Prohibition—including the authorities.

Now well heeled, Nelson returned to Chicago, where he caught the eye of blue-eyed Helen Wawrzyniak, a pretty 16-year-old salesgirl in a five-and-dime. Helen was impressed. At 5-feet-2 and 94 pounds, she was smaller than Nelson. Over her parents' objection, she married the guy in 1928 and stood by him through pretty rough times.

Two children were born, Ronald in 1929, Arlene the next year. But they cramped Baby Face's style. They were soon packed off to Nelson's mom, Mary Gillis.

Nelson robbed his first bank in Spring Grove, Ill., a piddling job in 1930 that paid him and his cohorts little. Next, came the First National Bank of Itasca, Ill., which encouraged the gang to hit a bank in Hillside, Ill., where Nelson shot a guard. The resultant heat caused the gang to split up.

Newspaper accounts of the Hillside stickup described one of the bandits as "a young man with a baby face." The name stuck, though Nelson hated it passionately. Helen thought it "cute."

On Jan. 15, 1931, Nelson was nailed by cops as he held up a jewelry shop off Michigan Ave., in Chicago. And during a lineup, he was recognized as the robber who had shot the guard in Hillside. That July 17 he was sentenced to one year to life in Joliet Penitentiary. A short time later he was linked to the Itasca bank heist and brought back to Chicago for trial.

Convicted, he was handed another one to 20 years. Nelson knew he had to escape now or never. After a train trip, as he was getting into a cab in Joliet for a ride to the prison—and while handcuffed to his guard and wearing leg irons—Nelson made his move. He pulled a gun from nowhere and escaped. How he got the weapon was never learned, though it was suspected his wife had it slipped to him on the crowded train. Baby Face never saw the inside of a prison again.

Back to San Francisco fled Nelson to link up with a dark-haired bootlegger named John Paul Chase, who later became his lieutenant. Chase gave something Nelson needed badly—hero worship. Prohibition's end found Baby Face and Chase in the Minneapolis area robbing banks.

On March 4, 1934, Nelson committed his first murder of record, an unexplained rubout of paint salesman Theodore Kidder, 35, in St. Paul. Baby Face was recognized, and newspapers splashed the story and his picture across their front pages. Off to Reno sped Nelson once more. In Nevada he pulled at least one contract murder.

But it was with the John Dillinger mob that Baby Face Nelson gained his greatest notoriety. Dillinger was a bit wary of the trigger-happy runt, but his gang had been reduced by arrests and killings. Nelson, like Dillinger, was totally fearless. He just enjoyed shooting people more.

They robbed a bank in South Dakota, another in Iowa during which Dillinger was shot in the shoulder. It was decided to lay low while the leader recovered, so the gang drove to the Little Bohemia Lodge on Little Star Lake in Northern Wisconsin. Primarily a summer resort, it was open all year. That April the gang had it all to themselves. The owner recognized them, of course, and got word to the Chicago office of the Criminal Division of the Department of Justice, forerunner of the FBI. On Sunday night, April 22, 1934, agents surrounded the lodge. The women hid in the cellar while the gang members slipped out a back window and escaped through the woods. Nelson stopped long enough to machine-gun to death agent W. Carter Baum.

Several days later, while still on the lam, Nelson, Chase and two of their ilk were pursued by three policemen in a patrol car. The lawmen cut off Nelson's car, but Baby Face got the drop on them with his tommy gun. He beat one officer to the ground and ordered the other two to start running. Then Nelson took aim at their backs. Only the pleading of his buddies that they were already hot enough induced Baby Face not to shoot. He was so frustrated, he shot out the glass of the police car.

But time was running out on desperadoes who rampaged across many states in those turbulent times. Congress had enacted laws permitting interstate pursuit of gangsters and making it a federal crime to carry stolen goods across state lines. In the end, their own notoriety proved their downfall.

Dillinger and Nelson & Co. pulled one more bank job, in South Bend, Ind., June 30, 1934. And then on July 22, outside a Chicago theater, Dillinger was cut down by federal agents tipped by the Lady in Red. With the rubout of Pretty Boy Floyd in October, Baby Face Nelson became the most sought-after criminal in the land.

On Nov. 27 of that same year, an informer notified police that Nelson was in the Chicago area in a Ford V-8 with Illinois plates 639-578. He was spotted in Barrington with his wife, Helen, and Chase. Two feds, inspector Samuel Crowley and Special Agent Hermann E. Hollis, roared after them.

At a crossroad outside town, about 4:30 p.m., battle lines were drawn, the lawmen's car about 50 feet from Nelson's disabled Ford. While Helen sought safety in a cornfield, Nelson opened up with his machine gun, Chase with a rifle. Crowley fired a machine gun, Hollis a shotgun. At one point Hollis saw Nelson's legs exposed behind his auto and let him have both barrels of heavy metal.

Screaming in pain, Nelson raced toward the feds, firing a long burst. Crowley emptied his magazine and then pitched forward into a ditch, mortally wounded. He died later in a hospital. Hollis, flopped across a fence, was found dead. More than 60 shots had been fired by the lawmen, an uncounted number by the outlaws.

Hit 17 times, Nelson escaped with Chase and Helen in the agents' car. He died at 7:35 p.m. in Helen's arms in a lonely hide-out. The faithful Helen later told reporters her husband had a smile on his face but tears in his eyes over leaving his two young children. It made nice reading.

The next day the body of the gunman, naked under a bloody blanket, was found in a ditch near Niles Center, 15 miles north of Chicago. Helen gave up two days later and was let off lightly for revealing the identity of Nelson's partner in murder. Chase was nabbed a month later on the west coast and sentenced to life in prison.

Dolls and Guys

Joseph McNamara
August 9, 1992

Beautiful and ruthless, Virginia Hill came out of the Alabama sticks to become a mob bag lady and TV celebrity at the Kefauver Senate crime hearings in 1951.

She liked poetry and had a nodding acquaintance with art, but her true love was hard cash.

Without the encumbrance of a job, Virginia was able to throw some of the most lavish bashes in New York and Hollywood. How? A little brown envelope that arrived weekly with crisp $1,000 bills inside.

How does one apply for these envelopes? Well, one has to be shapely, accommodating and able to play dumb to all inquiring lawmen.

The result, for Virginia at least, was four husbands and a succession of lovers, including Chicago's bookie king Joseph "Joey E" Epstein, tax expert for the Capone mob; New York's pride, Joe Adonis and Frank Costello; and Benjamin "Bugsy" Siegel, the gambler who absorbed gangland slugs at Hill's posh Beverly Hills home and still lives on the silver screen.

Virginia was born Aug. 26, 1916, in Lipscomb, Ala., the sixth of 10 children of Mack Hill, an itinerant handyman and lush. The family moved to nearby Bessemer, and their mother, Margaret, left Mack and got a job. Virginia, oldest of four daughters, cared for the brood until she was 17.

A voluptuous beauty with chestnut hair and the song of the South in her talk, she left for Chicago's World's Fair to become a dancer. But her fate was waitressing at a restaurant on the midway. There she was spotted by Joe Epstein, a myopic 33. He was smitten for life.

A small, balding man with a hawk nose, Epstein was not leading-man material. But he had more cash than Virginia thought possible. She moved in with him. It was Joe who sent the brown envelopes, even after Virginia moved on to greener fields.

Through Epstein, Virginia met other Chicago mobsters, including Frank Nitti, Tony Accardo and the Fischetti brothers. She also met Adonis, Costello and Lucky Luciano in New York. The hoods were impressed by Virginia's curves, but also by her quick mind.

She became Adonis' mistress in the 1930s, did considerable traveling. According to lawmen, she was a courier delivering money to syndicate leaders. She grew rich and began sending cash to her poor family.

It was as a giver of lavish parties that Virginia Hill first captured notice. In New York initially, later on the west coast, Virginia tossed $100 tips to waiters. Her dinners cost thousands.

Virginia would shuck her shoes and do a torrid rumba, her favorite dance. She was attracted to Mexican men, and married one.

Virginia made many trips to Mexico, and there were rumblings among lawmen that she was somehow involved in the drug trade. But she was never charged.

Nightly, Virginia traipsed Broadway with a dozen freeloaders. There was a brief fling as part owner of the Hurricane night club, 49th St. and Broadway, but she quickly got bored with it.

In 1938, Hill headed west, at Adonis' suggestion, and took an apartment in Hollywood. She was married to rumba dancer Carlos Gonzales Valdez briefly. She took a shot at the cinema, enrolling in a Columbia Pictures acting school. Despite dating Gene Krupa, John Carroll and Bruce Cabot, Virginia never made it in celluloid land.

But parties, yeah. One at Ciro's cost $4,800. Nightly at the Mocambo, she dropped more than $1,000.

Newspaperman Lee Mortimer tells of a World War II evening at Hollywood's Clover Club when Virginia was hosting 20 guests. An acquaintance of Mortimer, with a war-boom fortune, wanted to upstage Hill. He brought 40 people and ordered champagne. Because of shipping shortages, his guests were limited to domestic stuff, one bottle each. Virginia's people got the best imports, two bottles each.

It is not recorded when Virginia met Bugsy Siegel, the volatile and flamboyant hood whom Warren Beatty has portrayed on film. But the chemistry was right. She called the handsome mobster-gambler her "one true love."

Siegel, credited as the mob visionary who made Las Vegas a gambling mecca, built the first casino with millions in underworld money and called it The Flamingo, Virginia's nickname. It was a financial flop. Dealers and other personnel stole prodigious amounts by rigging games for friends or failing to report the proper take. Mobsters who had bankrolled the operation became unhappy, but Siegel stood up to them. He even told Luciano off.

Virginia lived a life of luxury. She wore designer clothes and $300 pairs of shoes. She leased a mansion on Linden Drive, had several apartments. Still the brown envelopes came.

Florabel Muir, a correspondent for the *Daily News*, reported spotting one of the envelopes when it arrived at the same beauty parlor both she and Hill frequented. The returnee's name was "Joey E."

"When Virginia showed, she opened the envelope at once," Muir said. "The girl doing her nails told me it contained 10 $1,000 bills."

Virginia and Bugsy began arguing over his attentions to other women. And in June 1947, she flounced off to Paris. That June 20, three carbine slugs tore through a window of Virginia's mansion and killed Bugsy instantly as he read a newspaper.

Some probers thought the syndicate had paid back Siegel for costing it money. But the case was never solved.

On returning to this country, Virginia told badgering reporters that Siegel was a poetry lover, the same as Virinigia.

Hill whammed the public in its electronic eye in 1951 when Sen. Estes Kefauver brought his Senate crime committee to New York for hearings. While millions watched on earlier-day TV, Virginia tossed wisecracks at the legislators.

She testified with a straight face that she never knew how Siegel or Adonis made money.

"They didn't tell me anything about their business," she insisted. "I don't care about their business."

About her own finances, the mink-draped Hill testified, "I take care of myself." But she gave no source of income beside "playing the horses."

In a private hearing, when ancient Sen. Charles Tobey of New Hampshire insisted on knowing how she got so much money, Virginia shot back that it was because she was sensational in bed . . . or words to that effect.

In a hallway, Hill decked the *New York Journal-American*'s Marjorie Farnsworth with a right and screamed at reporters: "You goddamned bastards, I hope an atom bomb falls on all of you."

After that, it was all epilogue for Virginia Hill. The IRS did not believe she made her fortune on the ponies, or on her back, for that matter. Their probe revealed she had gone through $500,000 in a decade and paid peanuts in taxes. They filed charges of tax fraud.

Hill married Sun Valley ski instructor Hans Hauser and escaped to Europe. She had a son, Peter, and settled near Salzburg, Austria. And while she cultivated a taste for Mozart, the IRS auctioned all the clothing, furniture and jewels she had left behind.

She chafed under the whispered Austrians' slur, "Frau Gangster," as Hauser did when he was addressed "Herr Hill."

On March 25, 1966, leaving a note that said she was "fed up with life," Virginia took sleeping pills and lay down in the snow to await death in the village of Koppl. She was 49.

A "Rat" Called Karpis

Joseph McNamara
April 27, 1986

He was called "Old Creepy" by the mobster buddy who knew him best. The feds called him Public Enemy No. 1. Top G-man J. Edgar Hoover called him a "rat." He called himself Alvin Karpis. And his arrest ended the crime career of the last of America's colorful desperadoes of the 1930s.

Pasty-faced and frail, he stood tall with a submachine gun in his clutches and earned the bloody purple of gangdom rule with 16 bank heists, four mail robberies, three kidnapings and four murders, by conservative estimate.

Canadian born, Karpis developed into an All-American thug, stopping his errant ways just long enough to become marbles champ of Topeka, Kan.

Francis Albin Karpoviecz was his name at birth in Montreal Aug. 10, 1909, the son of Lithuanian migrant parents. Sickly as a child, he was pampered by his parents and three older sisters and soon became a brat. When the boy was 12, a concerned doctor discovered a defective heart valve and advised plenty of rest. Francis made this a lifelong pursuit.

When he was four, he moved with his family to Topeka and 12 years later to the Chicago stockyard slums, as his unskilled father, John, sought better jobs. In Chicago, the pimply youth learned car stripping from Lester Gillis, another social outcast who blazed an outlaw career as Baby Face Nelson.

In 1927 his doting parents shipped him back to Topeka to live with a married sister, and cops there noticed a sharp rise in petty robberies. One night, the youth broke into a jewelry store and showed the effrontery or dull wits to try to pawn some of the loot in town. He was sentenced to 10 years in the state reformatory under the name he had given the judge, Alvin Karpis, a name he carried the rest of his days.

In the can, Karpis met Harry Barton, and the pair sawed their way to freedom and fled to Chicago. On March 23, 1930, the two were arrested in Kansas City for possession of safecracking paraphernalia and were returned to the reformatory. When, still later, Alvin was found with two knives, he graduated to the state penitentiary at Lansing. There, his life took a turn—he met Fred Barker.

Fred, the favorite son of Ma Barker, saw a kindred soul in Alvin, and they became friends. It was Fred, noting the piercing gray eyes and cold demeanor, who hung on Karpis the name "Old Creepy." After their paroles months apart in 1931, Fred brought Karpis to Tulsa to meet Ma, who took an immediate liking to him.

In Tulsa, Karpis married a coed, Dorothy Slayman, who took him for a jewelry salesman. Ma argued against the marriage, and Creepy left his bride after a few months, never to return. Dominated by Ma, Karpis became a member of her gang and in time a co-leader. After several jobs in Oklahoma, the Barkers moved to Missouri, where, in West Plains, Fred and Alvin killed their first prey, Sheriff C.R. Kelly, Sept. 11, 1931. Kelly recognized their car as a robbery getaway vehicle.

The gang quickly moved to St. Paul, Minn., and continued their robberies. When cops raided their rented apartment moments after Ma and Fred had fled, the bandits suspected Ma's current lover, Arthur Dunlop, had squealed. Dunlop's body was found with three bullets in it.

Now, the Barkers and Karpis rode roughshod. When an attorney they hired failed to show in court to represent a gang member, the bullet-sprayed body of the lawyer was found on the first tee of a Tulsa country club.

The Cloud County Bank in Concordia, Kan., gave up $240,000 to the gang, the Third Northwestern National Bank of Minneapolis $30,000 and the National Bank of Fairbury, Neb., $150,000.

In St. Paul, Karpis met Dolores Delaney, 19, who found in Old Creepy her kind of man. She became his moll. At the same time, Karpis convinced Ma Barker that a kidnap was the way to go. The Barker-Karpis gang settled on brewery executive William Hamm Jr., and on June 15, 1933, he was snatched from a St. Paul street. After the family paid $100,000, Hamm was released.

During a $30,000 payroll heist that August, one cop was killed and another wounded by the Barker-Karpis gang in South St. Paul. The caper was marked by a vintage getaway car equipped with ear-splitting siren and smoke screen, the brainwork of Shotgun George Ziegler, an ex-Al Capone employee.

On Jan. 17, 1934, the gang kidnaped bank president Edward Bremer, 37, in St. Paul and got $200,000 for him. But the gang slipped up. Despite Ma's admonition that the boys wear gloves, son Arthur "Doc" Barker took his off to light a cigarette, and he left an incriminating fingerprint on a spare gasoline can used in the car getaway. The G-men had a link to the gang.

Feeling the heat, Karpis elected to have "Doc" Joseph Moran, a one-time physician, change his features. Old Creepy had suffered a broken nose in a gang fight during his Lester Gillis days. Doc straightened it, altering Karpis' face somewhat. Surgery to change fingerprints failed. Doc liked to drink, and when he drank, he liked to talk. His weighted body was dumped into Lake Erie.

Now the gang scattered. Ma and Fred went to Florida, Karpis and Doc Barker to Chicago, where Doc was nabbed by the feds, who had traced ransom money to him. Karpis lit out for Hot Springs, Ark., and some fishing.

A map found in Doc's Chicago digs led the feds to a cottage on the shore of Lake Weir in Oklawaha, Fla., where Ma and Fred languished. Karpis, having moved to Miami with another gang member, Harry Campbell, visited the Barkers for some fishing. But Karpis and Campbell were back in Miami when, on Jan. 16, 1935, federal agents moved in and killed Ma and Fred in a four-hour, 1,500-round gun battle.

Karpis instantly bugged out for Atlantic City with his pregnant Dolores Delaney and Campbell and his girl, Winona Burdett, 22. Suspicious police issued an alarm for the Karpis auto, giving its license plate and model but neglecting to identify its occupants. So cops at the Jersey resort did not know what they had when they knocked on the door of a room at the Dan Mor Hotel.

"Stick 'em up, we're officers," one lawman shouted through the panel.

"Stick 'em up yourselves, coppers, we're coming out!" barked Karpis. He fired one shot through the wall into the next room to alert the two women. The slug struck Dolores in the leg, alerting her instantly.

With a roar of machine-gun fire, the two hoods burst out of the room and ran down a fire escape. There followed a wild 200-round surge of gunfire in the streets below that, amazingly, hurt no one, as the gangsters in a stolen car tried to find their way out of the maze of foggy, unfamiliar streets.

Karpis and Campbell escaped, kidnaping an Allentown, Pa., psychiatrist to Ohio to use his car. But time was winding down on Karpis. Already declared Public Enemy No. 1 since Baby Face Nelson had vacated that office, Karpis now sent word to Hoover that he was coming to personally kill him.

Hoover bridled and threw every available fed into the search for Old Creepy, who was traced to New Orleans through his interest in fishing. While agents staked out Karpis' hideaway, Hoover flew from Washington to personally arrest the "rat" on May 1, 1936.

Karpis was convicted of the Hamm kidnap and sentenced to life in prison. When Alcatraz opened its doors in Frisco Bay, Karpis was sent there. Shorn of his tommy gun, Old Creepy proved to be a wimp at the hands of more physical prisoners. In all, he spent 32 years in prison before his parole on Jan. 14, 1969. Ill and arthritic, he was deported to his native Canada. He was almost 60.

Karpis later wrote a book that emphasized two points: (1) Ma Barker was not the brains behind the gang, he was—she was a kindly soul just interested in "her boys," and (2) Hoover was a coward who needed 20 agents ringing Karpis' auto before he made the arrest.

Later Karpis moved to Torremolinos, Spain, where, on Aug. 26, 1979, at age 70, he was found dead of an overdose of sleeping pills in an apartment where he lived alone.

The Con Man of 1,000 Faces

JOSEPH MCNAMARA
MAY 6, 1984

On Dec. 10, 1926, some $129,000 worth of street markers arrived in Chicago from the Rochester Signal Co. of upstate New York. Piled high in a warehouse, the signs proved embarrassing. The Windy City's Bureau of Streets, it seems, knew nothing about the order. John Green, the firm's Chicago-area salesman, sheepishly explained that a Harry Delste, whom he had met outside the bureau offices, had convinced him that he had great influence in city affairs, and Delste later gave him the order.

Green's commission was $17,000, and he immediately peeled off $11,000 for Delste. Taken to a rogues' gallery at police headquarters, Green discovered sadly that Delste was really Joseph R. "The Yellow Kid" Weil. The suave, glib talker known to bunco squad cops nationwide as possibly the greatest con man in American history had struck again.

It was not too difficult. Weil had had lots of practice. He had sold gullible visitors several of the Loop's office buildings, which he did not own. He once sold the city's Masonic Temple. He sold Grant Park—three times. And on several occasions, he sold a half interest in all the yachts on Lake Michigan.

Who was this dapper, exalted swindler? Some people knew him as Sir James Ruskin of Wellington. Others as Herr Kokor Tourneur Saint Garriot, or Walter H. Weed, financier buddy of J.P. Morgan and oil magnate Walter Teagle. Still others knew him as Henri E. Geuel, Fellow of the Royal Society of Master Engineers, or Richard E. Dorane, Fellow of the Royal Society of Master Surgeons.

Under all these names, and many more, Weil was acknowledged, even among his peers, as the brainiest, slyest, most imaginative charlatan of the 20th century, who piled up an estimated $8 million, only to lose the whole boodle to yachts, fancy cars, ill-advised legitimate investments and a weakness for redheads.

Weil was born on June 23, 1875, in Chicago, not far from the area now known as the Loop. His merchant father was a civic leader with an active interest in politics. Young Weil shunned politics, though he obviously would have been good at it. Instead, he discovered Johnny Butterley's saloon, a famed watering hole on Broadway on Chicago's north side frequented by actors and safecrackers. Stage personalities Eddie Cantor, William Gillette and H.B. Warner hung out there, when in town. Ditto such silent screen luminaries as Charlie Chaplin, Wallace Beerry, Lewis Stone and Francis X. Bushman. Their studio was on nearby Argyle St. Weil listened to their shop talk, apparently picking up a flair for acting and costumery.

But it was the shady side of the law that beckoned alluringly to Weil. He found irresistible the flim-flam, the phony promoters, wiretappers and sundry crooks. Here he met two of the slickest con men in the business, Fred Buckminister, a former policeman, and Frank Tarbaux. In time, both worked for Weil, when he became the master.

There was the time Weil and Buckminister rented a vacant bank in Muncie, Ind., and filled it with con men as tellers and their girlfriends as patrons so they could sell it to some unsuspecting sucker. They even hired a streetcar motorman to act as a guard.

One look at the bustling activity, and the mark handed Weil the money. When he came several days later to take over his financial jewel, he found only a shuttered old hulk of a building.

The Yellow Kid drew his nickname from a cartoon character of the 1890s that he favored, and he was quick to capitalize on the moniker. He had yellow-reddish hair and a golden beard, drove yellow cars, handed out yellow calling cards and always wore yellow dress gloves.

He was sartorially elegant, loved Scottish tweed suits and pearl beaver hats with black velvet-lined coats. One of his favorite roles was that of Herr Koktor Tourneur Saint Harriot, for this make-believe called for a monocle with black ribbon. Oh, that monocle paid for itself a thousand times over.

One of Weil's earlier capers was one of his most inventive. With a former riverboat gambler named Jim Porter, Weil perpetrated what became known as the Great Michigan Free Land Swindle. The pair purchased some undesirable land at $1 an acre at the turn of the century. Weil introduced Porter as an eccentric millionaire who gave away free lots. Porter gave them to hookers, barkeeps, cops, anyone who would take one.

Weil would whisper to the dupes not to let others know about the good deal, but to be sure to register the land at the county seat. Now, as luck would have it, Porter's cousin was the registrar. And for the occasion he upped the registry fee from $2 to $30, splitting the take with his cousin and Weil. Porter and Weil made $16,000, and the suckers had no redress—they had paid nothing for the land.

Weil was by turns a counterfeiter, a fixer of horse races, a forger, an impersonator on a grand scale and a mail schemer. At one point, he bought his own brokerage house, so authentic, it was even equipped to make an honest deal, should the occasion arise. He phonied pedigree papers and sold 40 dogs for a profit of $8,000.

Weil's range was phenomenal. He was not above firing a shotgun loaded with gold dust pellets into the sides of an old quarry and then blithely selling stock in his new "gold mine."

Some of his scams were as elaborate as a Hollywood opus. To pass himself off as a copper and oil magnate from Jerome, Ariz., he faked letters from J.P. Morgan and Standard Oil's Walter Tegle, in which the two tycoons vied for Weil's mines. With such bait, Weil reportedly cleaned up $500,000 in phony stock certificates to the mines.

Weil was arrested some 40 times during his fabled career, but was sentenced only to four meaningful terms in the pen: One to 10 years in 1909 for a con game, serving 15 months; eight years in 1919 for conspiracy, being pardoned by the governor after four; five years on a federal rap in 1926; and a late 1930s term of 27 months for mail fraud.

In the 1926 case he was nabbed with $20,000 in bonds stolen during a 1924 train robbery in Roundout, Ill. Weil alibied in court that at the time of the crime he was busy fleecing $30,000 out of a judge, a parole board member and a lawyer, all from a state in the

Deep South. They would come forward and testify to this, he assured an incredulous judge. But the worthies did not show up. And Weil went off to the slammer.

The sentence did serve Weil in one way, though. It headed off prosecution on the Chicago street markers finagle.

Weil married in 1910 and had one daughter who, with her mother, tried for years to get him to go straight. But he never did, until he ran out of steam and retired in 1941 after his last jail term.

In 1948 Weil published an autobiography in which he said he took money only from those who could afford it and, in the process, taught them a lesson in honesty. For, he said, "each of my victims had larceny in his heart." One might get the impression Weil was doing society a favor, although he stopped short of saying that.

Bankers and lawyers were the most gullible, Weil felt, because they thought no one would dare sell them a bill of goods. And, he added, if the victim thought you were stupid, you were halfway home.

Somehow, Weil must have mastered the psychological weaknesses of potential victims. Explain, if you can, how—while being taken to Joliet Prison in Illinois after a swindle conviction—he was able to sell $30,000 in worthless stock to the detective guarding him.

In 1975, then a welfare patient in a Chicago convalescent home for two and a half years, Weil reminisced on the eve of his 100th birthday.

"If I had it to do all over again, I would be foolish if I didn't," said Weil, by now shriveled and frail. And in a commentary on the modern-day dupe, he added: "If anything, I would be raking in more money."

Of his last days, which ended Feb. 26, 1976, Weil said, "I still like to look at the ladies. I like to sip a wine now and then." And he appreciated the radio. But, added the man whose financial grafting had become legend, "I will not play bingo with the rest around here. It's a ripoff."

The Legendary Louis Lepke

JOSEPH MCNAMARA
DECEMBER 28, 1986

Of all the mob bosses raised to their illicit thrones and kept there by murder, only one died in the electric chair—Louis "Lepke" Buchalter. It was not the only distinction this caliph of crime had. Shy and soft-spoken, Lepke elected to infiltrate the legitimate commerce of garments, furs, baked goods and trucking, while his fellow hoods chose the more obvious lures of bootlegging, gambling and dope.

From 1928 to 1940, Lepke ruled a sinister gang that terrorized these industries in New York City. It was ironic that he bought the hot seat over the rubout of an almost unknown trucker-turned-candy man named Joseph Rosen. Of course, the fact that Rosen, 46, was about to tell special rackets prosecutor Thomas Dewey about how Lepke drove him out of the garment trucking business made Rosen stand tall in the eyes of the top hoodlum.

Rosen was blasted by three men in his confectionery store at 725 Sutter Ave., Brooklyn, Sept. 13, 1936, while a fourth kept the escape car humming at the curb. Fifteen slugs hit Rosen. He probably was dead before he hit the floor.

For several years the slayers walked the streets pursuing their murderous ways—it was newspapers that hung on Lepke's unit the term "Murder, Inc."—while Lepke, all 5-feet-7 of him, quietly ran his organization. Officials believe from the testimony of stoolies that the cadre, with Big Al Anastasia as top gun, snuffed out between 60 and 80 people on Lepke's orders.

Directing the unit was a rather unusual criminal. Buchalter was born in February 1897, on the lower east side, one of 11 children of hardware store owner Barnet Buchalter and his wife, Rose. The other 10 children went legit. And so did Louis—until he finished grammar school in June 1912.

To his impoverished mother, who sold food door-to-door, the future mobster was "Lepkelen" or Little Louis, which his cronies made "Lepke." Lepke ran errands after school—the only honest work he ever did—and dutifully turned in his $3 a week to the family fund. Lepke's father died when he was 13. His mother tried to keep the family together, but failed. Lepke struck out on his own.

At 18 he turned to crime with Jacob "Gurrah Jake" Shapiro. Shapiro was coarse, loud and flamboyant, while Lepke was quiet, doe-eyed and conservative. But the two were close as thieves for 30 years.

Lepke was bagged for a loft burglary in 1915, but the charge was dropped. The following year, he was nailed for stealing a salesman's samples in Bridgeport, Conn., and he served his first time. In 1918 Lepke went to Sing Sing for a year for grand larceny. Two years later he landed in the Big House again. By the time he got out, he was on the fringe of the big time.

He moved to center stage when Little Augie Orgen got his in a doorway Oct. 16, 1927. Also shot, but not killed, was Orgen's bodyguard, John Diamond, who later won villainy as Jack "Legs" Diamond.

Lepke brought a difference to the east side. Instead of using his thugs to terrorize the unions' opponents during strikes, Lepke worked them into the labor locals. Through threat and violence, they controlled the unions while keeping an eye out for Lepke's interests.

Union leaders, who had employed the head smashers during labor disputes, were chagrined to find them inside. Lepke used the same tactic on management, which also had used illegal muscle during strikes. For dissenters, there was acid in the face or bombs in the showroom.

For all his viciousness, Lepke skirted retribution. In 1933 he was arrested in an East 68th St. apartment for "vagrancy," but was freed when he produced $800 from his pockets. All this changed in 1935 when Gov. Herbert Lehman named the incorruptible—and ambitious—Thomas Dewey to dig into the city's rackets.

Now, the fear of aides being convinced by Dewey to give testimony became an obsession with Lepke. Potential witnesses were sent out of town, or killed. It was Lepke's paranoia that doomed Rosen.

"Rosen's shooting off his mouth that he's going down to Dewey," Lepke told his thugs, according to later testimony. And they carried out Lepke's hit orders.

The hitmen were Emanuel "Mendy" Weiss, Louis Capone and Harry "Pittsburgh Phil" Strauss.

Strauss killed about 30 people nationwide, according to underworld historian Will Balsamo, and he loved to shoot; his fellow gunman had to pull him off following a hit so they could escape.

The feds' and Dewey's net began to close in on Lepke. In 1937 he and Gurrah Jake were indicted for narcotics and antitrust violations. Lepke went underground.

Dewey called Lepke "the worst industrial racketeer in America," and he brought intense heat on the mob to shake Lepke from his hideout. Charles "Lucky" Luciano, in prison but still a major crime force, decided Lepke would have to be offered up. Through an intermediary Lepke trusted, he was induced to surrender to FBI director J. Edgar Hoover personally, on the understanding that "the fix was in."

But the minute Lepke got into Hoover's taxi, he realized he had been double-crossed.

Lepke was convicted on the federal raps Jan. 2, 1940, and sentenced to 14 years. Jake had already pleaded guilty. Handed over to the state, Lepke was convicted two weeks later in general sessions of extortion and handed 36 years.

But it was the chair that Lepke feared. In October 1941, Lepke, Weiss and Capone were tried for the murder of Rosen. The previous January, Abe "Kid Twist" Reles had fingered Lepke in the Rosen murder, as part of his singing about Murder Inc. and Brooklyn crime in general.

Reles later plunged to his death out of a window of the Half Moon Hotel in Coney Island while under police custody, under circumstances more than strange.

Several Lepke stalwarts testified at his trial. Sholom Bernstein, who noted his first name meant peace, said he had driven the getaway car when Rosen was done in. He said the hit was ordered by Lepke.

More damaging, perhaps, was the testimony of Max Rubin, a one-time teacher and ex-Lepke cohort. Three months before the slaying, Rubin had gone to Brooklyn at the order of Lepke to "try to straighten out Rosen," Rubin testified. He said Lepke gave the order to kill Rosen.

After the rubout, Rubin was sent out of town by Lepke, as were other possible witnesses to the crime. Rubin repeatedly pleaded with the mobster for permission to come back to his family. At one point Rubin met Lepke under an awning in a driving rain and the hood asked Rubin, "How old are you?"

Upon the answer "48," Lepke told Rubin, "You've reached a ripe old age."

A few months later Rubin was shot in the head on a Bronx street corner, but he lived to help drive the nail into his boss' coffin.

Lepke, Weiss and Capone were convicted of Rosen's slaying. Pittsburgh Phil was convicted and executed for another killing.

On the evening of March 4, 1944, Lepke followed Capone and Weiss to the electric chair in Sing Sing.

Lepke apparently had done some minor tattling, but not enough to save his hide. In an 11th-hour statement, read by his wife, Betty, Lepke assured the world in general and the syndicate in particular that he was not a stoolie.

The Mystery of "Mr. 880"

Joseph McNamara
December 25, 1983

The counterfeit bill was passed at a cigar store on Broadway near 102d St. And it cost the proprietor who accepted it, as bogus bills always cost someone. But the victimized cigar-store man was too busy running the shop alone to check the bill closely. Even if he had had the time, it was unlikely that he would have scrutinized the money. It was a dollar bill. Who checks for phony dollar bills?

It was November 1938, and the economy, with war in the offing, was moving out of the Great Depression. The queer bill was caught by a local bank, which charged the cigar vendor's account $1 and turned the offending item over to the Secret Service, that part of the Treasury Department entrusted with keeping the currency pure.

The bill was shipped off to the Secret Service laboratory in Washington for analysis, and a map was hung on the wall of the New York office of the bureau, with a red thumbtack indicating where the bill was passed—standard procedure when a counterfeit note is seized. A new file was opened for the miscreant and numbered 880.

As it turned out, the bill was historic. It was of ludicrously bad workmanship—the reworked portrait of George Washington would have fooled very few, and the numbers were fuzzy—and it was printed on ordinary bond paper available at any stationery store. Also, the feds realized no other counterfeiter in the United States at that time (and few in history) stooped to the production of phony dollar bills.

Other bogus ones were seized in the weeks and months that followed, mostly in and around Manhattan, though a few came to light in other boroughs and a few in New Jersey communities just across the Hudson River. According to the red-dotted wall map, most of the bad bills appeared on Manhattan's upper west side.

The most frequent victims were small store owners, bartenders, clerks at subway turnstiles, newspaper vendors and the like. Hundreds of bills passed through their hands daily, so that even when jolted by the phony money, they had no idea who had handed it to them.

Many people do not count their small change—how badly can you be ripped off for less than a dollar? So even bank tellers who would scrutinize a $50 bill would toss the old buckaroo right into the drawer. Soon the funny Washingtons began to turn up in bank accounts in the Midwest, the South and even on the west coast—until the awareness of the bogus ones tightened up bank procedures.

The feds had very little to go on. By the end of 1939, fewer than 600 of the clumsy ones had been passed, hardly enough to pay a counterfeiter for a year's work. And the rate was so slow that the Secret Service agents could not zing in and nab the counterfeiter in the act of passing his bills.

About this time, the Secret Service agents were chagrined to notice that some of the phony ones were appearing with the name "Washington" charmingly misspelled "Wasihngton." The Secret Service came to the painful conclusion that the counterfeiter, in trying to improve his product, had reworked the letters and reassembled them out of sequence. The most interesting thing about these bills was that they were accepted with the same alarming aplomb as the previous funnies. A few people who were seized passing the bills were victims who had just accepted them blithely themselves.

In January 1944, the Treasury felt constrained to warn New Yorkers about the blitz of bogus bills. At that time, most of them appeared under the serial number K 70025356 A and contained "several imperfections," according to the feds. George's eyes and hair were crudely rendered, and one eye appeared almond-shaped, the feds pointed out. Also, the front of George's shirt seemed to be soiled, and the small lettering around the Treasury seal was murky. But by now, Washington's name was spelled correctly.

As the years passed, the bills, all silver certificates, appeared in "J" series as well as "K," most of them on the upper west side, though occasionally Yorkville on the east side and Wall Street downtown got a break. By 1946, $4,027 in silly ones had been passed in New York, and by the end of 1947, more than 5,000 of the counterfeit bills had been spent. Then, on Dec. 4, 1947, fire struck a top-floor apartment at 204 W. 96th St., near Amsterdam Ave., and the mystery of 880 began to clear up. The blaze had begun in a pile of junk accumulated by the occupant, Edward Mueller, known to neighbors as "Pop."

Seventy-two-year-old Pop, a 5-foot-3, 120-pound, blue-eyed recluse, was often seen sifting through the rubbish piles of the west side for reclaimable junk. Balding, with a smattering of white hair over his ears, displaying a skimpy mustache and a toothless grin for everyone he met, this eccentric exponent of free enterprise would push a cart as he rummaged through the city streets.

Some of the junk would be sold to wholesalers. Some, especially toys, would be left outside his apartment door, where neighbors with children would help themselves. And much, it seems, would be stashed in his apartment.

Firemen responding to the blaze tossed large portions of the junk from the two-room apartment into an alleyway, where a developing snowstorm soon covered it. And Pop went off to spend that Christmas with a daughter in Queens. He had had a close brush with death: His dog had awakened him to the danger of the fire, but the animal perished.

It was not until Jan. 13, 1948, that two youngsters were able to take advantage of the thaw to poke through old Pop's junk in the alley. There they discovered two $1 bills and some plates for making them. The boys took the items to the W. 100th St. station house, where detectives John North and Louis Behrens recognized the bills as phonies.

Secret Service agents Sam Callahan and Thomas Burke were called in and found an additional $25 in bogus notes, several tubes of printing ink, some parts of a small hand press and negatives for Federal Reserve $10 and $20 bills. An additional plate for a $1 bill was discovered in a trunk in the cellar.

The $10 and $20 negatives had never been used, the agents determined, but the bogus $1s they quickly linked to their long-sought quarry—Old 880.

When Pop returned to the apartment Jan. 14, the feds nabbed him. It turned out his name was Emerich Juettner, although he was known as Mueller and also Miuller. His story was a fascinating one.

A native of Austria, where he had learned something about engraving, Juettner came to this county as a teenager, married and had two children. Among several occupations he pursued was that of a gilder of picture frames. For years, while raising his family, he lived on the east side, where he performed janitorial duties to offset his rent. After his wife died, he moved to the west side and began his career as a purveyor of junk.

"It was my way of making a living," the hawk-faced oldster explained to intrigued arresting agents.

But the living was not always easy. A proud man who had always provided for himself, Juettner pretended to his daughter and son that he was doing just fine. Actually, he was running off the ridiculous $1 bills on his hand press in his kitchen to provide food for his dog and himself and to pay his $25-a-month rent.

A story about the eccentric old counterfeiter by St. Clair McKelway in *The New Yorker,* caught the eye of 20th Century Fox, and a highly romanticized version of the story, with obligatory love fiction, was brought to the screen in 1950 in a movie called *Mr. 880,* featuring Edmund Gwenn, Burt Lancaster and Dorothy McGuire.

The real Emerich Juettner, dressed in layers of clothing, a screwdriver in his back pants pocket, a paint brush tucked into his dusty vest, was arraigned before U.S. Commissioner Garrett W. Cotter on charges of counterfeiting and possession of plates. It was his first brush with the law. Eventually, he was sentenced to nine months in prison.

"The capture of this man relieves the Secret Service of a terrific headache," Secret Service chief James J. Maloney said with remarkable understatement. He noted that "880" had eluded the law longer than any counterfeiter in United States history. A factor, according to agents, was Pop's "complete lack of greed." He ground out a buck only when he or his dog got hungry.

Prince of Pals

Joseph McNamara
June 28, 1992

"**M**a, dance with Pa," the short, full-faced young man in fancy duds urged.

The woman, weary but intensely interested in dancers at the festive wedding reception of a relative in Park Slope, Brooklyn, just sighed.

"C'mon, Ma, dance with Pa," her son persisted.

"I'm tired, Francesco," she replied quietly.

"Dammit, Ma, dance with Pa!" the now-infuriated man shouted as he yanked a pistol from inside his elegant silk suit and fired three shots into the dance floor.

Celebrants at the nuptial shindig looked in surprise. But the band played on. And Ma and Pa danced.

It was 1918, and Frankie Yale, not yet the Beau Brummel czar of Brooklyn racketeering, was clearly on his way toward having his demands followed precisely. In the 1920s he would cut a wide swath through the bootlegging and gambling empire of the city.

A killer, he could be charming. And he did help poor neighbors, a sort of Italian Robin Hood, though this in no way deterred him from his life's headlong pursuit of plunder.

The Prince of Pals, as he was called, was rubbed out July 1, 1928, by machine-gun fire as he drove his new Lincoln on a Brooklyn street. He became the first New York hood to succumb to the blast of a tommy gun.

Born Francesco Ioele on April 13, 1893, in the slums of Reggio, Calabria, Italy, he emigrated here in 1900 with his parents, Dominico and Isabella (Simone), his older brother Giovanni and his younger sisters, Rose and Catherina.

Another brother, Angelo, would be born in New York, according to underworld historian Will Balsamo, who had related the dance-floor tableau.

The family lived on the lower east side. Pa worked the East River docks and became a citizen in 1908. The parents were horrified to learn that the extortion of the Black Hand and Camorra they had hoped to leave in Italy was alive in this country, thanks to the relocated Mafia.

They were later saddened to discover that Francesco, though amassing wealth and power beyond their wildest dreams, also was a part of that sinister world.

In 1903 Dominico made a shoe-shine box and told 10-year-old Frankie to earn a few bucks. One of his customers was Johnny "Little John" Torrio, then 21 and leader of the James Street Boys.

Torrio liked Frankie and usually flashed him a $10 bill. The kid was impressed. He came to idolize Little John.

At 13, Frankie joined the Five Points Juniors, young ruffians aping their elders in the notorious 1,500-member Five Points Gang. At 15, he was swept into the senior gang because of his minor role in the slaying of a rival mob member.

In 1909 Torrio left for Chicago to be top lieutenant of his whoremaster uncle, Big Jim Colosimo. Before leaving, Torrio introduced Frankie to Alphonses Capone, then 10. As Torrio had taught Frankie the tricks of mobdom, so Frankie would teach Al Capone.

Frankie later gave Capone a job as bartender/greeter in his bucket-of-blood dance hall, the Harvard Inn, in Coney Island.

As Frankie became a proficient hood, he changed his name from Ioele to Vale to confuse lawmen. In time he became known only by another name, Frankie Yale.

Arrests for disorderly conduct gave way to busts for gun possession and even murder. But most counts were dismissed. The Ioeles moved to 66th St., Borough Park, Brooklyn, in 1915, and it was in that borough that Yale flourished.

The next year Yale formed a goon squad he would rent to both union and management at stiff prices in labor disputes. He set up the Yale Taxi Corp. of 125 cars and later bought a funeral home. He also owned a firm that peddled a five-cent stogie, a "Frankie Yale."

According to Balsamo, Yale became a blood-oath member of La Cosa Nostra the night of Aug. 10, 1916.

Prohibition made Yale wealthy, as it did many mobsters. He had fancy cars, expensive clothes. He wore a four-carat diamond ring and a belt buckle with 75 small diamonds.

Yale had been imported to Chicago by Torrio to knock off Colosimo because Uncle stood in the way of Torrio's expanding the bawdy-house operation into bootlegging. Again, in 1924, Yale was brought west to off florist Dion O'Banion, a Torrio-Capone foe. Yale shook O'Banion's hand while two other gunsels put him away.

O'Banion was given a magnificent funeral, the most elegant in Chicago mob history. It snared Yale's interest. Considering his line of work, it occurred to Yale he might be dusted off at any time. He told confederates he would like to get a flashier send-off than O'Banion's.

Yale's figuring was right. In 1925 he was shot and wounded as he drove home from a Coney Island speakeasy. On July 1, 1927, someone pegged a shot at him outside a Brooklyn cafe—but missed.

A year later to the day—about 4 p.m.—Yale was blasted as he tooled along 44th St. in the Homewood section of Brooklyn. A dark car with Tennessee plates overtook him, and four men inside opened up with pistols, tommy guns and a shotgun. Yale was shot several times in the head.

His auto careened onto the sidewalk and rammed a house, as the other car sped away.

Several motives have been given for Yale's demise at 35. The most reasonable is that Capone hit his mentor because Yale was knocking off liquor that Big Al had bought, then reselling the rotgut to the Chicago mobster for a second profit. Al suspected as much and sent James "Filesy" De Amato east in 1927 to find out.

De Amato was murdered, but not before he flashed word to Capone that Yale was indeed highjacking booze he was supposed to protect.

Yale got an anonymous note: "Someday you'll get an answer to De Amato."

It is believed that "someday" arrived July 1, 1928.

Yale got his wish. His funeral abounded in superlatives. He rested in a $15,000 silver casket. There were three priests at his funeral Mass in the Church of St. Rosalie, three more than at most Mafia requiems.

Tons of flowers—it took 38 flower cars to tote them to Holy Cross Cemetery. And mourners—there were 10,000. Some 250 cars formed the funeral cortege.

Something interesting happened at the funeral. Two Mrs. Yales showed up. There was Maria (Dellapia), whom he had wed on April 29, 1917, had two daughters by and divorced without her knowledge. And there was Luceida Yale, who had married Yale a year before his death.

Maria was recognized as Yales's rightful heir. But the estate of the Mafia chieftain with the fabled obsequies totaled just $7,982, of which more than $2,000 was in IOUs and debts of persons who could not be located, according to her attorney.

Fortunately, the great send-off to eternity cost the widow only $600. The rest was ponied up by pals of the Prince of Pals.

Yale's money worries are over, of course. Frank's been resting these many years in St. Edmund's section of Holy Cross Cemetery, in range 14, plot 9, under a tombstone marked by the family name, Ioele.

Queen of Crime

Joseph McNamara

November 24, 1991

G iven her early training, it is no wonder Sophie Lyons turned to an illicit buck. Given her beauty and her agile mind, it is not surprising that for half a century she was called the "Queen of Crime" by American lawmen.

Squeamish at the sight of blood, Sophie became a shoplifter, blackmailer and one of the most brazen of swindlers. Wife and sweetheart of bandits, bank robbers and gunmen, Sophie robbed on two continents with a flair that enabled her to rub elbows with royalty and top social figures.

Her imaginative approach to bank robbery made her infamous. Her audacity made her a legend.

In the 1880s, New York City police chief William Devery said, "Sophie Lyons is one of the cleverest criminals this country has ever produced."

And New York inspector Thomas Byrnes, in his 1886 book, *Professional Criminals of America,* called her "the most dangerous woman in the world."

Sophie lifted her first purse before she was six, and was arrested before she was 12. She could not read or write until she was 25. Yet she learned four languages. And in midlife—defying all odds—Sophie Lyons went straight, piling up $1 million from honest toil to replace the lost fortune she had made outside the law.

She was born Sophie Levy on Dec. 24, 1848, in a tough New York City neighborhood. Her father, Sam Levy, was a housebreaker.

Her mother, Sophie Elkins, was a pickpocket and a shoplifter. Both parents served jail terms, occasionally at the same time.

But young Sophie was proudest of grandpa Elkins, a second-story man in England. Said Sophie, he was "a cracksman to whom Scotland Yard took off its cap."

At an early age, the pretty girl was schooled by her mom in light-fingered crime. She once told a reporter, "All during my childhood, I did little but steal and was never sent to school."

With both parents in stir, Sophie came under the care of Federika "Marm" Mandelbaum, a storied fence of her day who gave the girl a postgraduate course in picking pockets. Sophie became her most adept pupil.

Once, when talking to other girls, Sophie got the notion that stealing was immoral. She told her dad, who was between jail terms. He promptly seared her arm with a hot poker to rid her of such ideas.

By the time she was 20, Sophie had served three jail terms. At 16, she was hauled off her honeymoon to serve one. She had wed Maury Harris, who boasted he was an ace pickpocket, a calling then considered the cream of the underworld.

But the cops were unimpressed with Harris' professed prowess. They nailed him red-handed, and he drew two years in the pokey. Sophie turned her attentions to Edward "Ned" Lyons, an English burglar 11 years her senior.

Ned was a powerful man with a thick red mustache. One of his ears had been bitten off in a drunken brawl. He was impressed with the young pickpocket with gentle gray eyes and auburn hair. Soon they were wed.

Ned, who pulled bank jobs in England and America, was in on the Ocean Bank robbery at Fulton and Greenwich Sts., Manhattan, with a take nearing $1 million. He bought Sophie a home on Long Island and insisted that she retire from crime.

This was a tall order for the young thief. When Ned was "at work," Sophie often went to Manhattan to lift wallets, jewelry and lace. At day's end, she would fence the stuff with Mandelbaum and return home to await her burglar hubby. In 1870, Sophie gave birth to a son, George, who, to no one's surprise, served much time for thievery and eventually died in his cell.

"Cut off in his prime," Sophie lamented.

Shortly after George was born, Sophie returned to her life of crime. She was arrested in Portsmouth, N.H., for picking pockets at a sprawling fair. Through histrionics—alternately weeping, trembling and blushing—Sophie convinced the police it was all a dreadful mistake. She was released and went back to the fair and swiped some more wallets and jewelry.

In 1871, Sophie was jailed for looting a New York jewelry store of diamond rings. Ned also was bagged, in a $150,000 safe looting. Both went to Sing Sing. Sophie helped him escape through a phony prison pass she obtained and civvy clothes smuggled in by a trusty. Ned walked out.

Later, Ned helped Sophie escape Sing Sing with a key from a wax mold the woman had furtively obtained.

Both fled to Canada. But on returning to this country, they were seized picking pockets at the Long Island Fair of 1876. They served out their sentences. Sophie, released first, decided to leave Ned. They had five children.

In the 1880s, Sophie reached stardom. With a new partner, Billie Burke, she robbed banks, shunning violence and insisting on guile and cunning. On one occasion she signaled Burke to slip into the rear of a bank and rob it while all the clerks were gawking at a circus parade out front.

Another time she induced a cashier, the only one in the bank at lunchtime, to come out to her expensive carriage while she, faking a broken leg, talked to him about opening a $10,000 account. Burke went in the back way and robbed the place.

Her take was enormous. She bought a townhouse in Manhattan, a villa on the Riviera and a ranch out West. She got tutors to teach her languages, art and literature. She moved in American society in Europe, using the aliases Mary Wilson and Fannie Owens. Her royal cohorts included the Prince of Wales.

Once, a gendarme grabbed her with her hand in a gentleman's pocket near the Arc de Triomphe. She was booked, to the shock of Americans in Paris. How dare the French arrest such a cultured lady?

They asked. The American ambassador demanded her release. The prefect of police apologized and gave her a police escort back to her hotel.

A short time later she robbed $500,000 in jewels from the high-society wife of Herbert Lorillard—in the same hotel. She got away with that one, too.

Back in America, Sophie blackmailed a wealthy Boston merchant for $5,000 after locking him in her hotel closet.

"Police will come for me eventually," he smugly said.

"Yes, and find you in my closet," Sophie cooed. "How will that look to your wife?"

The check was slipped under the door.

She was not so lucky when she tried the gambit on a Detroit public official. Sophie sat fetchingly on the horse block outside his home. The intended victim sprayed her with a water hose.

But Sophie's notoriety was putting her out of business, though she later claimed she had gotten religion. She married Burke and had a daughter by him. She made her honest money in Detroit real estate, she said.

Sophie spent much of her time trying to get criminals to repent. Her husband died in 1919, and she devoted her last years to providing funds for prisoners' causes and orphanages.

On May 8, 1924, she was visited at her Detroit home by three thieves she was trying to reform. They were more interested in Sophie's money than her advice. When she refused to hand over any cash, they beat her with pistol butts. She died of head injuries, ending an incredible life of 75 years.